United States of America, Why Have You Forsaken The One Who Empowered You?

EDNA L ISAAC

United States of America, Why Have You Forsaken The One Who Empowered
You?

ISBN: 978-1-938432-74-3 (paperback)

ISBN: 978-1-938432-75-0 (ebook)

Disclaimer

This book was assisted by AI.

Printed in the United States of America.

CONTENTS

THE CHARACTER OF A NATION

REV. JAMES A. GARFIELD

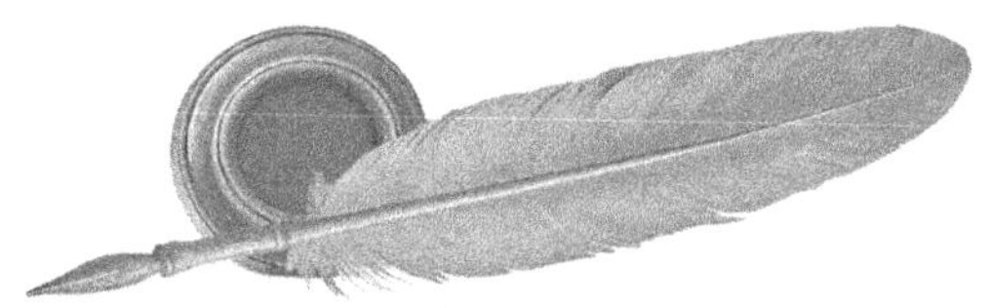

Now more than ever the people are responsible for the character of their Congress. If that body be ignorant, reckless, and corrupt, it is because the people tolerate ignorance, recklessness, and corruption. If it be intelligent, brave, and pure, it is because the people demand these high qualities to represent them in the national legislature.If the next centennial does not find us a great nation, it will be because those who represent the enterprise, the culture, and the morality of the nation do not aid in controlling the political forces."

—*Rev. James A. Garfield (1831–1881)*
President of the United States
Minister of the Gospel

ACKNOWLEDGMENTS

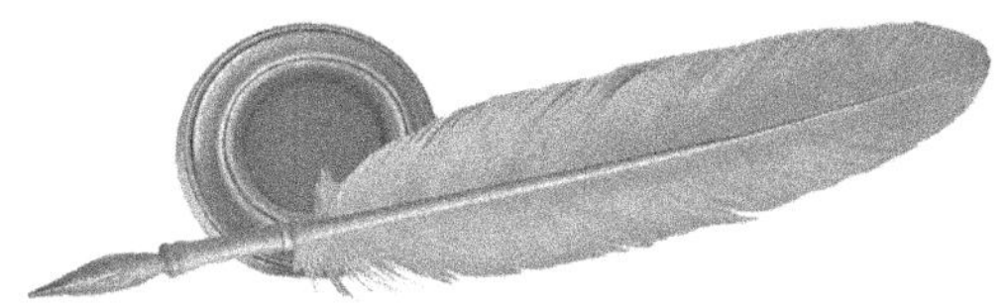

To God, First of All

I want to begin by giving thanks to God for His love and His mercy, for He has granted me the privilege of writing this book. I began it many years ago, but it was not until now that I was able to complete it. Today, I understand that God Himself preserved it for such a time as this.

To Tom Hughes

Alliance for Religious Freedom, LLC

I also wish to express my deep gratitude to Tom Hughes, president of Alliance for Religious Freedom, LLC. Without knowing me, and upon my request for Spanish material about our Founding Fathers, he generously sent me a package filled with valuable information that was of great help during the preparation of this book. I am immensely grateful for his collaboration and dedication. I recommend visiting his page to those who wish to be educated on these important topics.

On his website, he states the following:

> "When we, as a nation and its leaders, know, seek, and pray for the justice that God desires, according to the model of America's Founding Fathers (that is, our godly heritage), then God will respond to our obedience and faith in Him with blessing and rejoicing for our nation, just as He promised. Psalm 33:12 says, 'Blessed is the nation whose God is the Lord,' and Proverbs 14:34 says, 'Righteousness exalts a nation...'"

Blessings,

Tom Hughes

patriotpreachers@gmail.com

DEDICATION

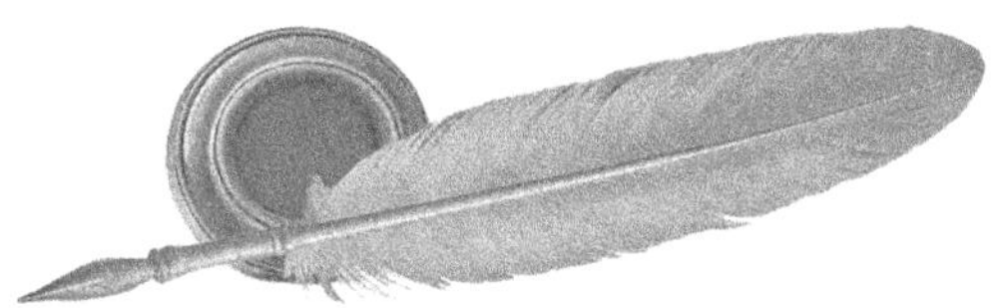

I dedicate this book with all my heart:

To my family, who have been my refuge, my strength, and my inspiration. Thank you for upholding me in prayer, for believing in me, for walking with me through every season, and for reminding me that God's calling is worth every sacrifice.

To the Church, my spiritual family, my brothers and sisters in Christ, who have been part of my growth, my formation, and my passion for the Kingdom. Thank you for being light in the midst of darkness and for keeping the flame of the gospel alive.

To the spiritual leaders whom God has placed along my path, who have sown into me words, vision, correction, and love. Thank you for teaching me to love the truth, to defend the faith, and to walk in integrity.

To the intercessors, pastors, evangelists, and anonymous servants who uphold this nation on their knees. You are the invisible heroes of the Kingdom. Thank you for not giving up, for not remaining silent, for not turning back.

And finally, to the most important One—to God, my Father, my King, my everything. To Him be the glory, the honor, and the power. He is the principal author of this book, the owner of my life, and the reason behind every word written.

May this book be a seed of revival, a trumpet of warning, and an eternal reminder that God still speaks, God still restores, and God still has a plan for this nation.

INTRODUCTION
MY HEART WEEPS

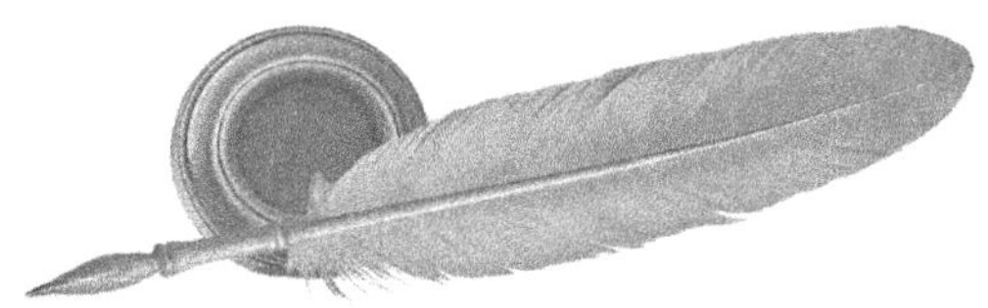

My heart weeps and breaks into pieces as I witness the destruction of my nation. *"Mi corazón llora y se rompe en pedazos al ver la destrucción de mi nación."* Vandalism fills the streets. Corruption permeates politics. Rebellious activists sow terror and intimidation. Innocent people lose their lives in a cultural battlefield—a war without limits, a struggle for conscience and common sense. We watch as the thirst for vengeance and the abuse of the defenseless advance cruelly, even stripping freedom from those who dare to oppose. Private property is destroyed as if it belonged to no one, and the law is distorted to protect tyrants while oppressing the vulnerable.

I began writing this book many years ago, but for some reason I could not finish it until now. I did not understand why God withheld its publication, but as I look at what is happening in our nation, I now realize that He Himself prevented me, because this message was reserved for this moment. Today I understand it, and I thank God for it.

I want to begin by telling you that on a day of deep intimacy with God, while enjoying our communion alone, He led me to read a portion of Scripture that brought me to tears. He showed me that we, here in the United States of America, one day—if Christ has not yet returned—will express those same words of pain and anguish that I read.

I have never been a negative or pessimistic person; on the contrary, I always try to find the best even in the worst. It is important for you to understand that when I wrote these words, we were living in times of peace, not the chaos we face today. Later, I will present the words of a people who experienced the wrath of a living and almighty God, who warned them tirelessly for years, yet they did not listen. As I read them, they remind me of the pride that dominates much of our nation.

In those days, as I began writing this book, I asked myself:

Will we one day speak in the same way when desolation and the judgment of God come upon our American soil?

Back then, I said we still had time—that a contrite and humbled heart is not despised by the Lord. Today, with everything happening in our nation, I ask myself: If we still humble ourselves, could God forgive the United States?

Let us look at what happened to God's people after He exhausted every option and gave them countless opportunities to repent, and still they refused. The Bible clearly warns us about the condition of the nations in the last days. Regardless of what we see, we must do our part so that God may have mercy.

When God's judgment finally came upon His people, after so many years of warning, Jeremiah acknowledged in Lamentations 3:22–23:

"Because of the Lord's great love we are not consumed, for His compassions never fail. They are new every morning; great is Your faithfulness."

Jeremiah was confronted within himself regarding the condition of his people and admitted that, despite everything they had done against God and His principles, His mercy had preserved them, at least a remnant. This book will lead you to confront yourself, today's reality, and the reality we will have to face.

I firmly believe that humility before God and repentance are America's only hope. Otherwise, we will be delivered into the hands of our enemies, and we cannot blame God for leaving us to their mercy, for He has been speaking to us for a long time, and we have not listened.

In Hosea 11:2–4 we see how God was moved with compassion for His people, who—though stubborn—He never stopped loving. They have always been, and will always be, the apple of His eye.

Later, God gave me a word that made me weep in His presence, revealing that we will experience the same in this nation if we do not confess, repent, and turn from our sins. Hosea 13 (RVR 1909) describes the consequences of rebellion, pride, idolatry, and spiritual blindness. It is a sobering reminder of what happens when a nation forgets its God.

When God gave me the title years ago, I thought it would be just another book on the subject, but now I know it is not. Although I am not pessimistic nor someone who sees judgment in everything, I believe in a God of love and mercy, and for that reason I must share what He gave me. That is why this book is now in your hands. I believe God's heart is grieved by what we have done as a nation; I even dare to say He is angry. We have despised His law, stained our testimony, broken His commandments, offended His heart, rejected His Word, and contaminated our spirit. When weighed on the scales of His justice, we have been found guilty.

Yet God is a God of love and mercy, and He can have compassion on us as He did with Nineveh when the entire city repented—though they later returned to their evil ways and perished a hundred years later. Let us not repeat their mistake. Let us remain humbled before His presence, for His mercies are new every morning. We do not need to fear, but we must be warned. If the thought of God's judgment on the nations terrifies you, remember that even if judgment comes upon this nation and the whole world, God will protect His children. And if we must depart, we will go into His presence. For us, to live is Christ and to die is gain. God has promises for those who love Him and await His coming.

My intention is not to cause fear, but to awaken in you a deep pursuit of the presence of God. May He reveal Himself to you in a special way. But it is necessary to mention that if even the people of Israel suffered the consequences of their rebellion, how much more will we? His Word is clear: He does not declare the guilty innocent nor the innocent guilty. Our iniquities as a nation will not go unnoticed.

What will we find in this book?

In these pages, we will learn how the United States of America became the great world power it once was—feared, admired, and respected. We will see what made the difference, how from a great crisis emerged a beautiful revival that empowered this nation, and what key turning point transformed its destiny.

Throughout human history, we see that when people humble themselves and the righteous govern, good things begin to happen. When leaders call the people to pray and seek the favor of the Lord, God hears from heaven and grants the petitions of His faithful.

Sadly, after that great moment in this nation, pride also came. We will examine what happened, where we stand today, and where the decline began. We will review how the enemy's evil plan infiltrated every area of society.

It is no coincidence that children disrespect their parents, that young people turn away from the faith, or that entire churches and communities fall into decay. All of it is the result of a strategic plan of the enemy to remove God from the human heart. Only those who have discernment and submit to God with humility can be protected from deception.

We will also address the greatest lie of the century: the supposed "separation of Church and State," and we will examine what our Founders actually said.

It is vital to educate ourselves and teach others their rights. We will see how we arrived at this condition, what statistics reveal, what the consequences have been, and what awaits us. But above all, we will see what God says. Have you asked yourself what will happen if you do not speak and do not teach your children—or the next generation—about the power, love, and plan of salvation of God?

What has the Church done?

We will analyze what the Church did to prevent—or allow—this deterioration. God's Word is fulfilled, but we must understand what happens when the Church becomes indifferent, remains silent, or embraces sin instead of confronting it. When the Church embraces false cults, destructive ideologies, and denominational pride, it enters a deep crisis that leads to spiritual suicide.

For this reason, we will explain how, when the walls are torn down and the foundation destroyed, the entire nation is in danger. When the foundations of a building collapse, the fall is inevitable. That is what has happened in this nation. Its solid foundations—rooted in the infallible Word of God, the immovable Rock of Ages—have been torn down, and now all that remains is to rebuild. But on what foundation will we rebuild? We cannot cover sin nor embrace hollow and deceptive philosophies that continue to infiltrate even the Christian community, where many have become apostates of the truth. We cannot allow destructive ideologies to govern the minds of our society while we remain with our arms crossed.

Chapter One

Urgent, America: What Is Happening to Us?

Let Us Awaken to Reality

Although I am a deeply positive person, full of faith, allow me—just for a moment—to lift the veil of hope so we can look directly at the reality unfolding before our eyes. What we are living in this nation is not a simple historical stumble. And if you still believe that the United States of America will return to that "normality" we once knew, I must tell you with sorrow that you are holding on to an illusion. No president, no leader, no human figure—no matter how noble their intentions—can reverse what has already been decreed from heaven. What a man sows, that he will also reap.

A Scenario That Is Not New

None of this is new. For decades, while many slept, destructive forces were silently shaping the mind of our society. They advanced without resistance, cornering us little by little, stripping away rights we once took for granted.

Today we see the fruit: overflowing hatred, multiplying lies, corruption in the air, a spirit of deception walking shamelessly among us. The "Reset." The Deep State. The New World Order. Conspiracies between governments and elites. Attempts at coups. Antifa. Movements of intimidation, terror, and violence. Apostasy within the Church. Satanic sects and twisted doctrines.

You have heard it. You have seen it. You have felt it. Perhaps you have even been part—consciously or not—of some of these phenomena. And although many prefer to look the other way, these realities reach us all.

A Silenced Society and a Church That Remains Quiet

What troubles me most is not the chaos, but the silence. I see people intimidated, unable to speak the truth for fear of repercussions. And even more painful: I see a Church that remains silent. A Church that watches but does not denounce. A Church that hides when it should rise.

I have never seen an environment so openly anti-Christian. The air is charged with hostility, vengeance, and corruption. And although these evils have always existed, today they feel different—heavier, darker. Because behind them operates a demonic force that presses relentlessly, while the spirit of the antichrist manifests in the highest spheres of power.

The Days Paul Announced

We are living what the apostle Paul described in 2 Timothy 3:1–5: "But know this: that in the last days perilous times will come..." It is no surprise; it is fulfillment. And although we must not fear, we must remain alert. You and I are watchmen. We are the voice that warns. We cannot remain silent. The trumpet is about to sound. Christ is coming. The King is coming. And if we once believed it, now we see it clearly: our redemption is near.

A Generation Marked by Signs

Jesus spoke of signs. He spoke of birth pains. He spoke of a generation that would see all these things and know that the end is near. That generation is ours. No other has seen what we are seeing. None has witnessed such precise, accelerated, and evident prophetic fulfillment.

An Experience That Sealed My Spirit

About seven years ago, while praying alone in the church, longing for a word from heaven, I felt as if two angels approached with urgency. Between them, a divine presence enveloped me. And I heard a phrase that shook my soul: "The end is near." I wept intensely. The Holy Spirit ministered to my heart and reminded me of a message that has almost disappeared from our pulpits: Christ is coming soon. I remembered Yiye Ávila and asked myself: Where are those who proclaim this message today?

The Spiritual Contamination That Sickens the Church

One of the deepest wounds in our society is born within the Church itself. Many no longer preach the true Word. The more "scholarly" some become, the further they drift from the essence of the gospel. And the gospel is simple. Pure. Direct. Without embellishment.

This confusion has left many without a spiritual compass. Many no longer know what to believe or whom to listen to. But God still has a remnant—a people who do not negotiate the truth.

A Nation Falling and a Church Distracted

Corruption has become scenery. People without a solid doctrine recognize what is happening and warn others. Meanwhile, those who do know the truth are distracted, entertained, lulled under a spirit of stupor. Blindfolds of darkness cover their eyes. They do not see. They do not discern. They do not speak.

Many have been so intimidated that they focus only on social causes, forgetting that the root of the problem is spiritual. We must return to speaking clearly. Without fear. Without filters. Without negotiating God's principles.

• • •

The Struggle for Power and the Invisible Hand of Heaven

The struggle for power we see today is the vilest this nation has ever witnessed. The well-being of the people no longer matters; only the agenda matters. And whoever does not submit is attacked.

While studying at one of the most prestigious universities in the country, I found a World Health Organization manual stating that by the year 2020, the United States would have a universal healthcare system. A plan written years earlier. A global design. An agenda crafted by men who play at being God.

But they forget something: in heaven, there is a God seated on His throne. He allows—up to a point. And when sin reaches His presence, He judges.

Corruption in Washington, in the media, and in major tech companies has opened a Pandora's box. Political, religious, and governmental scandals have become a global mockery. It is not new that they attempt to take global control; what is new is that now they do it without disguise.

An Unexpected Leadership and a Greater Purpose

Many hate the current president, but they cannot deny that his arrival was unexpected. He was not supposed to win. And yet, he won. I do not agree with everything he says nor how he says it, but I recognize that he was courageous. He confronted the Deep State. He did not bow. He exposed what others hid. And that has a price.

Do you understand now why he is so hated? Because he was the only one who dared to challenge the corrupt machinery of Washington.

Now he lives his second term in the midst of a fierce war. But whether we like it or not, God is allowing things that are part of a greater plan. He will give this nation according to what it has sown.

A Call That Cannot Wait

America, wake up. God has spoken. God has warned. God has extended His mercy. But a nation that turns away from its Creator inevitably reaps the consequences.

The normality we once knew no longer exists. The ground has shifted. The structures have changed. The spirit of the age has changed. But God does not change.

This is not a time to fear, but to awaken. Not a time to hide, but to rise. Not a time to remain silent, but to proclaim the truth with boldness.

The Church was not called to be a spectator, but a light. Not called to imitate the world, but to transform it. And if there was ever a moment to recover our position, it is now.

America needs an awakened Church. A Church that prays. That discerns. That confronts sin with love, but without fear. That does not negotiate the truth. That remembers who her God is.

Although darkness seems to advance, the final word does not belong to man, nor to governments, nor to elites, but to Almighty God.

God is still seeking men and women who will stand in the gap, who will lift their voices, who will not be ashamed of the gospel, and who are willing to be instruments of His glory in this final hour.

This chapter does not end in despair, but with a certainty: God is not finished with America. But America must return to God.

And to understand how we arrived here—and how we can return to the foundation that once sustained us—we must look back: to our Founding Fathers, to the principles that gave life to this nation, and to the hand of God that raised it.

Only when we remember where we came from can we discern where we are going.

Chapter Two
Your Right to Vote: What Many Ignore

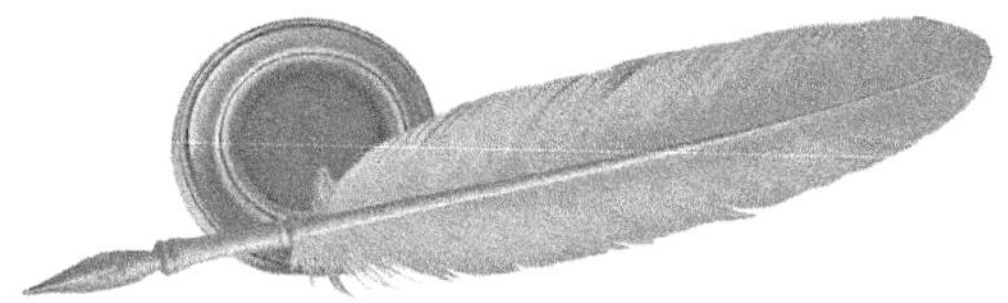

I would like us to continue this conversation with realism and common sense. Before moving forward, I want to clarify a very significant point and raise a question that perhaps we have never asked ourselves before reaching the conclusions we repeat or hear. Have you ever wondered why, if the territories of the United States were already inhabited, they never became what they eventually became until our Founding Fathers arrived?

We will answer this question later, but it is important to make clear that we do not deny the reality that, before the arrival of the Founding Fathers, there were already inhabitants in these lands. However, the point we will analyze here has become a major controversy, because today many want to rewrite history according to their political, social, or cultural preferences. Sadly, information is being taught based on ideologies rather than facts. We do not deny reality, but we cannot change history. We can debate all we want, but erasing evidence will never be possible. That is why it is our responsibility to educate ourselves and learn the most relevant information, especially regarding historical matters. If we do not educate ourselves, we will be easily deceived.

It is heartbreaking to see how the pillars upon which this nation was founded crumble more each day. We are undoubtedly living in chaotic times. Violence, destruction, deception, and corruption continue to increase, and with them, the disintegration of society. Morality, values, and common sense seem to belong to the past. Those principles that once shaped us into responsible, respectful, and committed men and women are now seen as obsolete, harmful, or distorted. They are ignored or manipulated by a small group of individuals who wish to advance their own agenda, regardless of whom they harm in the process.

We cannot ignore or neglect our right to vote. Every election year brings decisions that will affect the future of our children and our nation. Therefore, in addition to praying for discernment, we must use common sense when voting, just as our Founding Fathers commissioned us to do.

I had never been interested in politics, especially because I always heard a negative connotation surrounding it. I had not learned anything about it because, honestly, I was not interested. I thought politics had nothing to do with me. How wrong I was.

The worst part is that many people still think the same way. I remember that in my family, we used to say, "We are PNP" or "We are POPULAR," and the whole family voted for that party without truly knowing who we were voting for. We exercised our right out of tradition, without caring who the candidates were. When I discovered whom I had voted for all those years, I was shocked by my own ignorance. That was when I understood that, without knowing it, I had gone against the will of God according to Scripture.

I asked God for forgiveness and committed myself to educating myself before voting. I decided not to be influenced by dirty politics, manipulated media, or people who try to convince us with ideas that seem beneficial but ultimately destroy us morally, economically, and spiritually. I thank God that I came out of political illiteracy. Today I have an independent mind that is not manipulated by any party. I pray to vote for whomever God places in my heart—not out of tradition or pressure. God taught me that He does care who governs our cities, because it has never been His intention for the wicked to rule.

What Did Our Founding Fathers Think?

Three historical quotes from our Founding Fathers reveal profound truths that today seem forgotten:

Reverend Frederick Douglass, minister of the gospel and civil rights leader:

"I have one great political idea... The best expression of it I have found in the Bible: 'Righteousness exalts a nation, but sin is a reproach to any people' (Proverbs 14:34). This is my politics: the negative and the positive, and the whole of my politics."

John Jay, Chief Justice of the United States:

"Providence has given to our people the choice of their rulers, and it is the duty, privilege, and interest of our Christian nation to select and prefer Christians for their rulers."

Reverend Francis Grimke, minister of the gospel:

"If the time ever comes when the United States collapses, it will be because it has lost sight of the fact that 'righteousness exalts a nation, but sin is a reproach to any people.' If it does not maintain these fundamental principles, the United States will be nothing but a covenant with death and an agreement with hell."

Today, we see with our own eyes that what they warned about is exactly what has happened. The history of our Founding Fathers has been severely altered. If we do not study original history, we will believe the errors and lies being taught today. We have been told that politics and religion cannot mix, that pastors cannot speak about politics from the pulpit, and many other unconstitutional things.

But because we do not know the law or history, we allow ourselves to be deceived.

We have even been led to believe that ministers cannot participate in elections, when in the early days of this nation, it was precisely ministers who influenced the most important decisions. If you visit the State House, you will see portraits of ministers involved from the very beginning. The participation of godly men was common, and because of that, this nation was blessed.

That is why the Constitution of the United States has endured for so long. But I do not believe it will last much longer if the nation continues turning its back on God. When a nation abandons God, God eventually—because of His justice—gives it over to the consequences of its own path.

This is why choosing wisely is so important. When we do not pray, do not research, and discourage others from voting, we contribute to the deterioration we see today.

The Voice of the Church and the Imposed Silence

In a letter titled *"State Church vs. Free Church,"* Tom Hughes explains how the influence of pastors and Christians was essential to the existence of this republic. Early ministers taught that the Bible addressed every aspect of life, including civil government. They were even asked to preach sermons before legislative sessions to guide the creation of laws.

Many pastors served in Congress. Reverend Peter Muhlenberg helped draft the Bill of Rights. Could it be that the First Amendment—"Free Exercise of Religion"—was placed first to protect the voice of pastors?

However, in 1954, the Johnson Amendment silenced the pulpits by restricting the political participation of churches. Although this law violates the First Amendment, many churches submitted voluntarily, becoming state-controlled churches.

Today, 90% of pastors acknowledge that the Bible speaks about current social and political issues, but only 10% dare to speak about them.

This silence has left a moral vacuum that others have filled with destructive ideologies.

The Need to Participate

Many Christians have demonized politics, believing it is of the devil. But politics is simply the vehicle through which a person reaches a position of government. The problem is not politics; it is who occupies it.

God has used imperfect rulers to fulfill His purpose: Joseph, Moses, Deborah, David, Esther, and Daniel. Why would He not use men and women of God in positions of authority today?

. . .

When we say, "I don't vote for anyone," we are abandoning the responsibility God gave us. Remember Saul: he was not God's choice, but the people's. David was the divine choice.

If Christians do not vote, they cannot complain about the consequences.

Romans 13:1 reminds us that all authority comes from God. And God gave the American people the opportunity to choose their rulers. But when a nation abandons Christian values, it stops choosing according to God's heart.

That is why we are where we are.

An Unavoidable Call to Responsibility

America stands at a decisive point. This is not a moment for indifference or spiritual comfort. It is not a time to hide our heads or repeat empty phrases like "they're all the same" or "my vote doesn't make a difference." That mindset is precisely what has allowed others—with agendas contrary to God—to take positions of authority while the Church watches from a distance.

God did not call us to be spectators. He called us to be light, salt, influence, voice, conscience, and witnesses of His truth in the midst of a confused generation. And although many want to convince us that politics is "dirty," the reality is that dirt advances when the children of God abandon the territory that belongs to them.

The enemy does not rest. He understands the power of influence, of laws, of governmental decisions. He knows that whoever controls culture controls the minds of the next generations. And what about us? Will we remain asleep while others write the future of our children?

Voting is not a simple civic act. It is a spiritual act. A stewardship act. An act of obedience. An act of responsibility before God. Because when we choose rulers, we are not only choosing policies—we are choosing the moral, spiritual, and cultural direction of a nation.

Our Founding Fathers understood this. The ministers of old understood this. The prophets of Scripture understood this. And today, God calls us to understand it as well.

We cannot continue handing over government to those who despise truth, trample justice, and promote laws that destroy life, family, and freedom. We cannot continue justifying apathy with religious excuses. We cannot continue saying "God is in control" while ignoring that He gave us the responsibility to choose. God is in control, yes. But He will also hold us accountable.

History is watching. Our children will watch. And God is watching.

America will not fall because the enemy is strong, but because the Church is indifferent. It will not be destroyed by darkness, but by the absence of light. It will not be defeated by the sin of the world, but by the silence of God's people.

This chapter does not end with a simple call to vote. It ends with a call to awaken—to assume our responsibility, to recover lost ground, to remember that God gave us a voice, a conscience, and a duty.

Because when the people of God rise, history changes. When the people of God pray, heaven responds. And when the people of God vote according to righteousness, the nation is preserved.

America can still be restored. But only if the people of God decide to act.

CHAPTER THREE
CULTURE OF HATE

The time has come for Christians to vote for honest men and to take a consistent stand in politics, or the Lord will curse them... Christians have been extremely guilty in this matter. But the time has come when they must act differently... God will bless or curse this nation according to the course Christians take.

—Rev. Charles G. Finney (1792–1875), Revivalist of the Second and Third Great Awakenings, University President

As I watched the 2016 presidential elections—so close, tense, and fiercely contested—I was horrified by what my ears heard day after day. It seemed unbelievable to witness how far we had fallen as a nation in the realm of the media. I firmly believe those were the most malicious elections I have ever seen in my lifetime. I wondered how we had sunk so deeply, losing without remorse the values that once distinguished us and the social morality admired by so many nations.

I felt ashamed to think that the United States had become the laughingstock of the world. It pained me deeply to recognize the irony: from being a powerful, respected, and imitated nation, we had become the opposite. Watching television, I could not believe the paid advertisements created solely to discredit opponents, treating them as mortal enemies. I watched as they demoralized one another without compassion, and the consequences fell not only on them but also on their families.

I asked myself: Why not focus on the good each one desires for the nation instead of destroying one another with insults, accusations, and slander? But the worst part is that we call this "politics," participating without hesitation in defamation, manipulation, and deceit.

I was astonished by the hurtful, offensive, hate-filled words they hurled at each other. They sowed suspicion, distrust, hostility, and disrespect in the hearts of Americans. I watched one candidate hide behind a mask of apparent concern for the nation, but when I researched their life to make my decision, I was shocked by the injustices committed and how justice itself seemed to mock their actions. Even American lives were lost due to their irresponsibility, while that person enjoyed their family under immunity.

On the other hand, I saw how the other candidate was attacked for having a strong personality. Before running for office, many admired him as a wealthy celebrity. But once he revealed his conservative agenda, he immediately gained thousands of enemies who, to this day, have made his life impossible. We cannot deny that his way of speaking was sometimes uncomfortable, but over time one realizes he is not the monster many want to portray. If we look at Scripture, God used a pagan king named Cyrus, and yet He called him: "My servant Cyrus." Who are we to judge by appearances alone?

I was stunned to see how past mistakes were used as weapons to destroy candidacies. The candidates became objects of mockery, contempt, and public humiliation, and even their young children were ridiculed by the media. Character assassination—this monstrous force that stains reputations —was unleashed without restraint. These elections were, without a doubt, the most malicious I have ever witnessed. And for that very reason, I have never liked politics. The worst part was that the masses were confused, unsure of whom to vote for, because the nation lacked solid leadership.

What surprised me most was seeing how the upper class, educators, professionals, Christians, and people who consider themselves "cultured" fell into mental manipulation by the influences surrounding them. Without realizing it, they were dragged by a spirit of rejection, bitterness, and hatred, falling into the trap of division and strife.

In 2016, entire families were divided over politics. Organizations crumbled under pressure. Hatred was planted in children who did not even understand what was happening but were contaminated by the arguments of adults. As "intelligent" as we claim to be as a nation, we became puppets of mass movements, carried away by subtleties and empty words that profit nothing.

I thought we had learned the lesson of 2016, but we had not. In every election we repeat the same pattern—only deeper, with more violence, more hatred, and more intolerance. Today, if someone notices you think differently, you can become their worst enemy. Hatred has polarized our nation to such a degree that many can no longer see anything positive in those who do not share their school of thought. And the saddest part is that adults are modeling this behavior while our youth and children imitate it.

Social media does not inform clearly; it hides truths according to political preferences and destroys reputations without mercy. How did we reach this point as a society, where only the rights of those who think alike are respected?

If we look at history, we will see that this is not new. Before, it was done in secret, but today the shamelessness is so great that they no longer hide. They take pride in sowing hatred and indifference, even in the minds of children.

We ask ourselves: When did we lose common sense? The answer is simple: when we removed God from the most important spheres of society, especially public education.

In the past, our children were taught principles that taught them to respect their parents, authority, and God. Today, the lack of respect is alarming.

Benjamin Rush, signer of the Declaration of Independence and one of the leading advocates for public schools, understood that education without the Bible was incomplete education. Today, nothing resembles what he envisioned.

His vision was clear:

> *A nation without moral and biblical education is destined to collapse.*

And that is exactly what we are witnessing.

The Bible says:

> *"The fear of the Lord is the beginning of wisdom." (Proverbs 1:7)*

When we do not allow God's wisdom to guide our minds, we give place to foolishness. Psalm 53 confirms it:

> *"The fool says in his heart, 'There is no God.'"*

We cannot sow hatred, suspicion, and disrespect and expect positive results. Many Christians have fallen under the mental control of the media. Instead of praying, researching, and seeking direction from the Holy Spirit, they allow themselves to be carried away by their favorite political party, without considering the spiritual implications or asking: What does God say about this?

Today, we live in a diluted Christianity, molded to convenience, bearing no resemblance to God's original design. God does not change. His principles do not change. What He abhorred thousands of years ago, He still abhors today.

Isaiah 55:6–8 calls us urgently:

"Seek the Lord while He may be found..."

My eyes fill with tears as I recognize how deeply we have failed God—even those of us who bear His name. If we are honest, we will see that we have a spiritually weak, confused, and deceived generation that does not know the power of God. A generation that has created its own "god"—a permissive one, molded to personal preference, without holiness or reverent fear.

So how do we return to common sense? How do we recover the authority we have lost? How do we once again influence the world as God intended from the beginning?

The answer is simple and profound:

> ***Returning to the foundations.***
> ***Returning to the fear of God.***
> ***Returning to the infallible Word.***

You and I must make a decision. ***The first option*** is to allow the media and the masses to control our minds and the minds of our children, removing God from our hearts. ***The second option*** is to rise up, fight for our families, and leave a legacy worthy of the calling with which the Lord has called us.

I hope you choose the second.

Beloved reader, we have reached the point where we can no longer pretend that "everything is fine." It is not. And the most alarming part is that many—even within the people of God—continue walking as if nothing were happening, as if the moral, spiritual, and social decay surrounding us were simply "part of modern life."

No. This is not normal. This is not progress. This is not social evolution. This is spiritual collapse.

A nation does not fall overnight. A generation does not become corrupt suddenly. People do not lose common sense by accident.

It all begins when God is removed from the center. When His Word is replaced with human schools of thought. When truth is exchanged for opinion. When holiness is replaced with convenience. When sin is embraced, and correction is despised.

And that is exactly what we have done.

We have raised a generation that does not know God because we ourselves stopped teaching Him. We have allowed the media to educate our children while the Bible gathers dust. We have allowed hatred to become normal, division to be celebrated, immorality to be applauded, and truth to be ridiculed. And now we ask why we are where we are.

But here is the truth no one wants to admit:

> *The culture of hate we see on the outside is the reflection of the lukewarmness we have allowed on the inside.*

We can no longer blame the government, the parties, the media, or society. Responsibility begins at home. In the family. In the Church. In the heart of every believer.

God will not restore what we ourselves continue destroying through indifference. God will not heal what we are unwilling to acknowledge. God will not intervene while His people remain silent, divided, and asleep.

The time has come to awaken.
The time has come to repent.
The time has come to return to the Word.
The time has come to reclaim lost ground.
The time has come to stop being spectators

and become participants in God's
purpose for this nation.
Because if we do not do it, who will?
If we do not do it now, when?
If we do not do it for our children, for whom?
History is watching us.
Heaven is watching us.
And God will hold us accountable.

As I mentioned—and now reiterate—it is impossible to keep sowing hatred and expect to reap peace. We cannot keep sowing indifference and expect to reap revival. We cannot keep sowing silence and expect to reap justice.

The time to act is now. The time to return to God is now. The moment to lift our voice is now.

Because if we do not, we will not only lose a nation... We will lose an entire generation, as we are already seeing. And that, beloved reader, would be the greatest tragedy of all.

Chapter Four

The Founders: The Cost of the Freedom You Enjoy Today

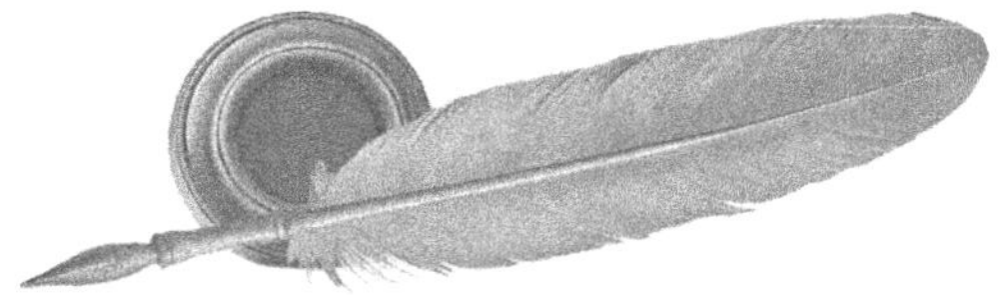

One of the most admirable characteristics of the United States of America is its welcoming spirit. For generations, this nation has opened its doors to millions of people from all over the world. Men, women, and entire families have arrived seeking what is known as the "American Dream": a better life, opportunity, freedom, and prosperity. Even the Founding Fathers were immigrants. They left England, fleeing religious persecution and seeking the freedom that had been taken from them. That is why most of us who live in this nation today—or our ancestors— came here with the same longing: a better life.

However, today, a growing debate exists. Many argue that modern historians, influenced by liberal ideologies, have attempted to remove God from America's history. And sadly, they have largely succeeded. They have rewritten history, planting in the minds of our children an anti-patriotic sentiment and a distorted view of our origins. The most lamentable part is that many have remained silent, naively hoping that "things will get better."

A Nation Born as a Religious Refuge

According to the Library of Congress, in its article *"Religion and the Founding of the American Republic,"* many of the colonies that formed the United States were established by men and women who fled Europe to worship God freely. New England, New Jersey, Pennsylvania, and Maryland were conceived as "plantations of religion." Most colonists did not come for economic reasons, but for spiritual ones. They wanted to worship God according to their conscience, without the oppression of the state church.

Even colonies like Virginia—initially planned as commercial enterprises—were led by men who considered themselves "militant Protestants," committed to the prosperity of the Church. But this truth is rarely taught today.

The History We Are Not Told

When speaking of the Pilgrims, people almost always mention Thanksgiving superficially, but they omit the essence of their mission. It is rarely taught that they had a clear and defined purpose: to establish a nation where the freedom to worship God would be the priority. God could have chosen any other place for them to begin the plan they had prayed over, designed, and entrusted to Him; however, it was here, in America, where He sovereignly set His gaze to bless it, prosper it, and bring the spiritual and material abundance we enjoy today.

Did individuals come among them who stained history? Of course. As in every era—yesterday and today—the enemy always attempts to infiltrate and sow destruction. But let us not repeat incomplete narratives or unfounded opinions. Go to the correct sources, educate yourself, investigate, and then form your own judgment. Otherwise, you will be easily deceived.

The original document of the Pilgrims states it without ambiguity:

> *"For the glory of God and the advancement of the Christian faith."*

They were not speaking of institutionalized religion. They were speaking of the gospel of Jesus Christ—a relationship with God based on biblical truth.

Today, atheist and liberal movements attempt to discredit these roots. But history cannot be erased. The original documents remain, testifying to what truly happened.

I believe we should be grateful that God chose this nation. We do not applaud the negative, but neither can we ignore the countless blessings we have enjoyed for hundreds of years. Do not allow others to plant hatred in your heart toward the land where you have been so blessed. On the contrary, seek the peace and prosperity of this nation, so that you and your family may also live in peace.

A Journey Guided by God

Before arriving in America, the Pilgrims spent years in Holland preparing spiritually. They studied the Word, strengthened their faith, and trained to establish a nation founded on biblical principles.

They attempted to leave several times but failed. They were persecuted, imprisoned, despised, and stripped of everything. But they did not give up.

Finally, their ship drifted... and arrived exactly where God wanted them to arrive. It was not a coincidence. It was not luck. It was divine sovereignty.

God brought them to this land to fulfill His purpose.

The First Ministers and the Foundation of Government

When the Pilgrims arrived in 1606, among them were Christian ministers such as Robert Hunt, Richard Burke, William Memase, Alexander Whitaker, and William Wickham. These men were fundamental in the formation of the House of Burgesses in 1619, the first legislative assembly in Virginia.

Contrary to what is taught today, it was the ministers of God who influenced the most important decisions. They provided spiritual guidance to the colony. They established moral principles. They taught the Word.

The history of the United States is saturated with Christian faith from its very foundations.

The True Origin of Thanksgiving

Catherine Millard, in *A Children's Companion Guide to American History*, explains that in 1623, after the harvest, the governor of Plymouth declared:

> ***"Gather to hear the pastor and give thanks to Almighty God for all His blessings."***

Years later, Congress proclaimed national days of thanksgiving, publicly recognizing Jesus Christ as Savior and asking forgiveness for the sins of the nation.

George Washington wrote in 1795:

> ***"It is our duty to acknowledge our obligations to Almighty God..."***

Abraham Lincoln declared in 1863:

"We have forgotten God... We have imagined that our blessings were produced by our own wisdom... It is appropriate that God be solemnly recognized by all Americans."

How is it possible that today, people claim these men were not Christians?

The High Price of Your Freedom

Do you know the real cost of the freedom you enjoy today?

- Tears
- Hunger
- Disease
- Sleepless nights
- Persecution
- Imprisonment
- Bloody wars
- Men and women sacrificed
- Innocent bloodshed

All so that you and I could live in freedom.

The United States has been the only nation to maintain the same Constitution for more than 246 years. Its secret? It was founded on biblical principles.

But today we live in a post-Christian era. Many have chosen to turn their backs on God. And when a nation rejects God, God gives it over to the consequences of its own path.

Education: The Beginning of the Decline

The first universities—Harvard, Princeton, Yale—were founded to teach the Bible and prepare ministers. Education was infused with Christian principles. Children learned to read using Bible verses. Science was taught as evidence of divine creation.

Today, however:

- Occultism is taught
- Satanism is promoted
- Immorality is normalized
- Faith is ridiculed
- Children are indoctrinated with destructive ideologies

And many parents remain silent.

God will hold us accountable.

How Did We Get Here?

Because we removed God from:

- Schools
- Government
- Family
- Culture
- Conscience
- The heart

And when God is not at the center, chaos takes His place.

An Urgent Cry

How must God's heart feel when He sees us like this?
We have allowed ourselves to be contaminated.
We have allowed ourselves to be deceived.
We have allowed ourselves to be lulled to sleep.

And meanwhile:

- Our children are lost
- Our youth are taking their own lives
- Our homes are destroyed
- Our nation is collapsing

How long?

Wake Up, America

Wake up! Wake up! Wake up!

Come out of the sleep of indifference. This is about your children. Your grandchildren. Your legacy. Your faith. Your nation.

Do not allow others to govern your way of thinking. Do not allow the media to educate your children. Do not allow lies to destroy what God has raised.

Many men gave their lives so that you could be free. Will you allow that freedom to be lost?

The United States is going from bad to worse. Its fall as a world power is imminent if it does not repent. But there is still a faithful remnant. There is still hope... if the nation humbles itself.

Join me in the next chapter. There, we will discover whether there is still a path to America's restoration.

Chapter Five

The United States: The Great World Power

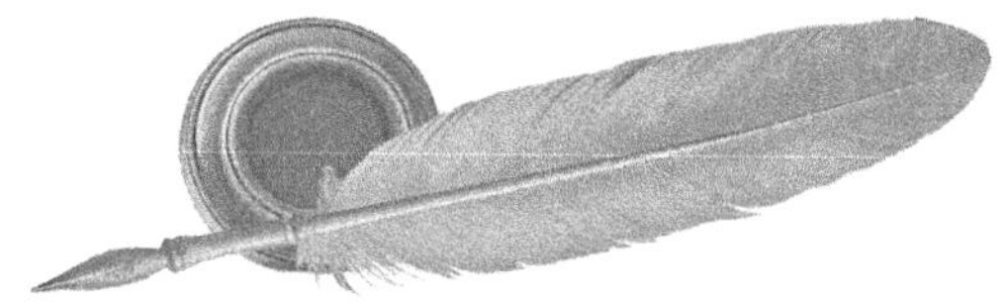

The Empire Born of Providence

If we study the history of humanity, we will see that every empire goes through three organically unfolding stages: its birth, its moment of glory, and its fall. The United States is no exception. This nation experienced an extraordinary rebirth—a period of splendor that led it to become the most influential power in the world. But that rise was not accidental or coincidental; it was the result of principles, sacrifice, and a deep dependence on God. Although today the nation remains influential, it is no longer respected as the greatest power, for moral decline has caused it to falter.

A Nation Born with Divine Purpose

If you have ever taken the time to study the original documents that shaped this nation, you will notice that the hand of God is present in every line. The United States did not arise by accident; it was a divine appointment with the Creator to preserve, influence, and govern among the nations. God had a plan, and for that reason, He chose God-fearing men to establish the foundations of this land.

To understand this more clearly, let us revisit the Declaration of Independence—a document that reveals the spiritual and moral essence that gave life to this nation.

The Declaration of Independence: An Act of Faith and Courage

The Founders were not mere revolutionaries crafting political schemes. They were men convinced that God had given them the right—and the duty—to establish a just and free government based on eternal principles.

In the Declaration of Independence (July 4, 1776), we find statements that today many may consider "politically incorrect," yet they reveal the truth of their faith:

- "All men are created equal."
- "Endowed by their Creator with certain unalienable rights."
- "Appealing to the Supreme Judge of the world..."

- "With a firm reliance on the protection of Divine Providence..."

The Founders recognized that freedom was not a gift from the king, the government, or men. Freedom came from God. And they were willing to risk everything—life, fortune, and honor—to defend it.

God Honors Those Who Honor Him

The more I study this document, the more evident it becomes that God supported these men. Their intention was clear: to found a nation that honored God and advanced the Christian faith. For that reason, God prospered them, protected them, and raised them as a world power.

But the Word of God also warns:

"I will honor those who honor Me, and those who despise Me shall be lightly esteemed." (1 Samuel 2:30)

The United States was honored because its Founders honored God. But if this nation chooses to turn its back on Him, God will also allow it to face the consequences.

The Remnant That Sustains the Nation

I firmly believe that the only thing holding back the full weight of God's judgment on this nation is the faithful remnant that cries out day and night. Otherwise, history would look very different.

But just as the remnant of Israel had to witness God's judgment upon their nation, the time will come when we, too, will see the consequences of collective sin.

Monuments That Speak: Faith Engraved in Stone

In *The American Patriot's Bible* (Dr. Richard G. Lee, 2009), monuments in Washington, D.C., are documented that testify to the Christian faith of this nation. Although many today attempt to erase God from public life, the stones continue to speak.

Washington Monument

- At the very top is engraved:
  - **"Laus Deo"** (Praise be to God).
- On its walls appear phrases such as:
  - "Holiness to the Lord."
  - "Search the Scriptures."
  - "Train up a child in the way he should go..."

The Capitol

- Above the House of Representatives:
  - **"In God We Trust."**
- A relief of Moses among the great lawgivers.
- Paintings of *The Baptism of Pocahontas* and *The Embarkation of the Pilgrims.*
- In the Capitol chapel:

○ George Washington in prayer beneath the phrase **"This Nation Under God."**

The Supreme Court

- The Ten Commandments are engraved on doors, walls, and sculptures.

Jefferson Memorial

- "God who gave us life gave us liberty."
- "I tremble for my country when I reflect that God is just..."

Lincoln Memorial

- "That this nation, under God, shall have a new birth of freedom."

These monuments are not decorations. They are silent witnesses of the faith that gave life to this nation.

Education: The Beginning of the Decline

For the past 80 years, the educational system has attempted to systematically eliminate every trace of Christianity. Original books were replaced with secularized versions. Children no longer learn true history. And the Bible—once the foundation of education—was expelled from the classroom.

But Scripture warns:

"The fear of the Lord is the beginning of wisdom."
(Proverbs 1:7)

As long as the United States sought that wisdom, it prospered. When it abandoned it, its decline began.

From Misery to Prosperity: The American Revival

There was a time when the United States was submerged in poverty and despair. The Great Depression devastated the nation. Wealthy men took their own lives. The country was in ruins.

But God raised leaders who, even in the midst of chaos, turned their hearts back to Him. And God responded.

After World War II, the United States experienced more prosperity and advancement than in the previous 400 years. It became the most powerful nation on the planet.

Why? Because its foundations were solid. Because it honored God. Because faith was part of its DNA.

How Did It Become the Great World Power?

The United States became a world power because it:

- Honored God.
- Founded its laws on biblical principles.
- Valued freedom as a divine gift.

- Educated its children in the Word.
- Recognized God's sovereignty over the nation.
- Had leaders who feared God.
- Maintained a sense of moral responsibility.

As Winston Churchill said:

"Responsibility is the key to greatness."

The Empire at the Crossroads

Every empire has three stages: its birth, its moment, and its fall.

The United States has already lived through its birth. It has lived its moment. And now it stands at the crossroads that will define its future.

If this nation continues rejecting God, its fall will be inevitable. But if it turns its heart back to the Creator, it may yet experience mercy.

The question is not whether God can restore the United States.

The question is: **Does the United States want to be restored?**

A Nation at the Edge

The United States became the great world power not by chance, but because it honored God. Its foundations were solid, its vision clear, and its dependence on the Creator evident in every document, every monument, and every monumental decision.

But now, this nation stands at a critical point—a point where empires decide their destiny, a point where history pauses... and watches.

Because every nation that rises without God falls.

And every nation that rises with God but later abandons Him falls even faster.

The United States is at that crossroads—between mercy and judgment, between restoration and collapse, between repentance and pride.

And although a faithful remnant still sustains this nation with its prayers, the question that echoes in the spirit is inevitable:

How much longer can a nation that has forgotten the God who raised it endure?

The monuments speak.
History speaks.
The Bible speaks.
But are we listening?

The chapter ahead is not just another chapter. It is a chapter that confronts, that exposes the spiritual reality, that reveals what many prefer to ignore—why the United States is losing what once made it great.

If Chapter 5 showed us **how** we became a world power, Chapter 6 will show us **why we are ceasing to be one**.

Prepare yourself.

What comes next is not comfortable, but it is necessary.

- It is not soft, but it is true.
- It is not political—it is spiritual.
- It is not opinion—it is a warning.

And like every warning from God, it comes with an opportunity:

- An opportunity to awaken.
- An opportunity to repent.
- An opportunity to rebuild.
- An opportunity to return to the foundation.

Join me in Chapter 6.

There we will see what happens when a powerful nation turns away from the God who empowered it...

And what can still happen if it chooses to return to Him.

CHAPTER SIX

THE SILENCED CHURCH: THE DANGER OF REMAINING QUIET IN TIMES OF CRISIS

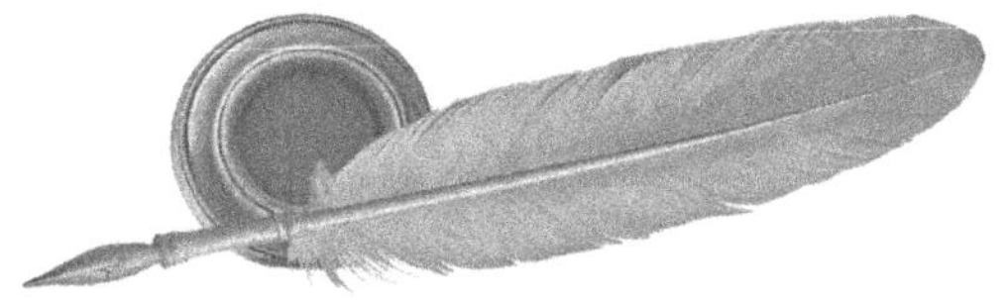

Reverend Martin Luther King Jr. expressed a truth that transcends generations: *"What concerns me is not the wickedness of the evil, but the indifference of the good."* That phrase is a mirror for our nation... and for the Church. For decades, modern historians have attempted to erase God from America's history. They have rewritten books, distorted facts, and planted in the minds of our children an anti-Christian sentiment. And the most painful part is that the Church has remained silent. Not only have we allowed others to define our history, but many within the body of Christ have embraced narratives without questioning their authenticity. Indifference has become a weapon that the enemy has used to advance without resistance.

Indifference That Opens the Door to Evil

MLK was not a perfect man—none of us are—but his fight for equality was deeply rooted in the Word of God. His movement was not sustained by human ideologies, but by spiritual convictions. Today, however, many want us to believe that the Founding Fathers were narcissists with no interest in equality. Historical truth shows the opposite. From the beginning, many of them attempted to abolish slavery but faced opposition. Although they could not accomplish it immediately, they established it as a future goal… and fought until it was achieved. They were not perfect, but they were visionaries. They were not gods, but they were men guided by God.

When the Church Is Silent, Others Speak

Our Founding Fathers fought so that what they suffered under the monarchy would never be repeated in this new nation. They sought a government where:

- No group would dominate the others
- Freedom would be protected
- Justice would be impartial
- God would be honored

Today, however, we see the opposite. We have allowed a culture of hatred to develop so deep that the well-being of the people no longer matters—only the agenda of a few. Whoever disagrees is treated as an enemy. It is the perfect strategy to silence those who think differently. And the Church, instead of being light, has remained silent.

While We Sleep, Others Legislate

While many believers sleep spiritually, legislators work day and night to pass laws that contradict our values. Some proposals have been just one vote away from:

- Banning Christian books
- Censoring religious messages
- Limiting freedom of speech
- Restricting biblical teaching

What once made this nation strong—faith, the Bible, religious freedom—is what many now seek to prohibit.

Presidents of the past founded Bible societies, funded missions, and promoted the Word of God. Today, many leaders seek to silence it.

The Intimidated Church and the Muzzled Pulpit

Tom Hughes expressed it clearly in his historical analysis: the American Church has gone from being the prophetic voice of the nation to becoming a state-controlled church—governed by fear, ignorance, or convenience.

Many pastors fear speaking out:

- For fear of losing members
- For fear of criticism
- For fear of being "politically incorrect"
- For fear of losing tax benefits

But the truth is this:

God does care about politics.

Because politics determines laws.
Laws determine culture.
And culture determines the heart of a nation.
Politics is simply a vehicle. The problem is not politics. The problem is who drives it.

Ignorance That Costs Freedom

Many Christians have never read the Constitution.

Never studied the Bill of Rights.

Never investigated their freedoms.

That is why they believe lies.

That is why they are intimidated.

That is why they remain silent.

The First Amendment—summarized—guarantees:

- Freedom of religion
- Freedom of speech

- Freedom of the press
- Freedom of assembly
- Freedom to petition

The very "monsters" criticized today were the ones who fought so that you and I could enjoy these freedoms.

Silence Is Not Neutral: It Is Complicity

When the Church is silent:

- Lies advance
- Injustice becomes normalized
- Truth is weakened
- Freedom erodes
- The enemy gains ground

Silence is not neutral. Silence is complicity.

God did not call us to be spectators.
He called us to be light.
He called us to be salt.
He called us to be a voice.
He called us to be watchmen.
A silenced Church is a weakened Church.
A Church that remains silent,
Is a Church that surrenders.
A Church that fears is
A Church that loses authority.
A Church that becomes comfortable

Is a Church that fades.
But there is still hope.

God has always worked with remnants—with small groups of men and women who refuse to remain silent, with hearts that burn for truth, with voices that cannot be bought or intimidated.

This is the moment to rise.
To recover our voice.
To defend truth.
To teach our children.
To pray... but also to act.
To be the Church Christ called us to be.
Because if the Church does not speak, who will?
If the Church does not rise, who will rise?
If the Church does not defend truth,
Who will defend it?
The future of this nation does
Not depend on politicians.
It depends on the Church.
It depends on you.
It depends on me.
It depends on people willing to say:
"We will not remain silent."
Prepare yourself for the next chapter.
Because what comes next,
Not only reveals the problem...
It reveals the path to restoration.

Chapter Seven

When the Walls Fall: The Price of Abandoning the Foundation

One night, God showed me a vision. In my vision, I was walking through the streets of the United States, but when I looked down, there was no solid ground. No streets, no structures, no foundations. Only rubble, ruins, and fragments of what had once been firm. I jumped from broken pieces, trying to move forward, but there were no bases holding anything together. Beneath my feet were only abysses, cliffs, emptiness. We walked as best we could over the remaining fragments. In that moment, the Holy Spirit began to minister to my heart and said, **"This is the condition of this nation's foundations."**

The foundations that once held the United States firm are no longer stable. They have been destroyed by the storms of immorality, sin, humanism, spiritual contamination, the silence of the Church, and the indifference of those who claim to love God. Only rubble remains.

If the Foundation Is Destroyed, Everything Collapses

The reason this nation was so blessed and empowered was because its foundations were rooted in the Word of God. Scripture confirms it repeatedly: ***when a nation acknowledges the God of Israel, it is blessed.***

The men who influenced the formation of this country loved God. They sought justice, equality, and truth. They were chosen instruments to bring blessing. But when the Church stops influencing society with the gospel, society loses the essence that keeps it as light in the midst of darkness.

Jesus said we are the light of the world and the salt of the earth. But if the light does not shine and the salt loses its flavor, what good is it?

That is what has happened in the United States. The influence of Christianity ceased to be part of government, culture, education, and public morality. And when the light goes out, darkness advances without resistance.

We cannot turn our backs on the One who made us prosper and then expect more blessings. Man believes he can succeed without God, but when he turns away, his life—and his nation—loses meaning and heads toward destruction.

Walls Torn Down, Society in Ruins

The walls that once held our society together have been torn down. In the desperate pursuit of "happiness," man has forgotten the only One who can give it. In the attempt to please everyone, he has gone against God—the only One who can give life and prosperity.

They have despised the Author of life. They have forgotten that He created all things and still holds control. They have played at being "gods," but have found only emptiness, confusion, and failure.

And the Church, contaminated by hollow philosophies, has become cold, superficial, and without discernment. A Church that no longer knows how to distinguish between truth and lies. A Church full of human ideas but empty of the presence of God.

THE SPIRIT OF INDOLENCE

If you are part of the people of God, listen carefully: spiritual indolence is destroying the Church.

God showed me that this spirit has paralyzed many believers. Indolence is the root of apathy, spiritual laziness, lack of commitment, indifference to the suffering of others, and the absence of passion for souls.

. . .

Jeremiah 48:10 says:

> ***"Cursed is he who does the work of the Lord negligently..."***

This is not about being theologians. It is about understanding simple truths that transform lives, families, and generations.

Isaiah 61:1 declares that the Spirit of the Lord is upon us to:

- preach good news
- bind up the brokenhearted
- set captives free
- open spiritual prisons

God has already given us the complete package. He gave us His Spirit, His Word, and His authority. But many do not use it.

Why Don't We See the Promised Victories?

If we have the Holy Spirit, the Word, and the resources, why don't we see the results?

Because indolence has put many to sleep:

- They do not evangelize
- They do not pray
- They do not intercede
- They feel no burden for souls

- They do not commit
- They do not grow spiritually
- They do not obey the calling

Many are ashamed to say they are Christians. Others spend years in church without maturing. Others are content to attend but not serve. And meanwhile, the world is perishing.

God Confronts Indolence

When I cried out to God, asking why so many Christians remain stagnant, He spoke clearly: **"Indolence has entered My people."**

Indolence:

- desensitizes
- numbs
- paralyzes
- extinguishes passion
- steals purpose
- halts God's prophetic plan

Many are so comfortable in their spiritual sleep that they do not want to wake up.

The Mandate Still Stands

Mark 16:15–18 is clear:

"Go into all the world and preach the gospel..."

It does not say:

- "If you have time."
- "If you feel prepared."
- "If no one criticizes you."
- "If you are not embarrassed."

It says: **GO.**

And it promises:

"These signs will follow those who believe..."

Signs do not follow spectators. They follow the obedient.

The World Preaches... and the Church?

Today, thousands of voices preach:

- immorality
- adultery
- fornication
- violence
- confusion
- destructive ideologies

Meanwhile, many Christians are content to sing within four walls, growing spiritually overweight but without impacting the world. The spirit of indolence has silenced many. And while we remain silent, the enemy speaks.

Eradicating Indolence: A Spiritual Urgency

To eradicate means to eliminate completely something harmful.

Indolence:

- affects your life
- affects your family
- affects your church
- affects your nation

Eradicate it:

- with the Word
- with prayer
- with obedience
- with repentance
- with action

Confess your sin. Close doors to the enemy. Renounce spiritual laziness. Wake up.

Beloved brother or sister, this is the moment to awaken. Shake off the sleep of indifference. Renounce the spirit of indolence that has hindered your growth and your calling.

God has equipped you. God has anointed you. God has sent you.

Do not live for yourself. Do not lock yourself in your own world. Do not ignore the pain of those around you.

Share your testimony. Speak of what God has done for you. Extend your hand. Be light. Be salt. Be a voice.

God will not put you to shame. He will back every step of obedience.

Because when the Church awakens, the walls rise again. When the Church acts, the nation finds hope. When the Church humbles itself, God heals the land.

The Walls Have Fallen... But Not All Is Lost

Symbolically speaking, the walls of this nation have fallen—the fundamental base that sustained it for so many years. But not all is lost. God always begins restoration with a remnant. And you are part of that remnant.

The walls have fallen. The foundations are in ruins. The nation that once shone as a beacon of freedom now walks upon spiritual, moral, and cultural rubble. And although this reality is painful, it is not the end.

Every time God allows the walls to fall, it is not to destroy... it is to awaken. It is to shake. It is to call His people back to the foundation they abandoned.

Because when the walls fall, what truly sustains a nation is exposed. And what sustains a nation is not its buildings, its economy, or its military power. What sustains a nation is its relationship with God.

The United States did not fall for lack of resources. It fell for lack of repentance. It did not fall for lack of opportunities. It fell for lack of obedience. It did not fall for lack of blessing. It fell for lack of foundation.

But here is the truth, the enemy does not want you to understand:

God always begins restoration from the ruins.

He does not need intact walls to raise a nation. He needs surrendered hearts. He does not need perfect structures. He needs a willing remnant. He does not need crowds. He needs one who says: **"Here I am."**

Chapter 7 showed us how we arrived at this point. Chapter 8 will show us what happens when a nation abandons God... and what can happen if it chooses to return.

Because even though the walls have fallen, God is still God. Even though the nation is wounded, God is still the healer. Even though the Church has been silenced, God is still calling. Even though the enemy has advanced, God still has the final word.

Prepare to enter Chapter 8. It is not a chapter to read lightly. It is a chapter to read with an open heart, with discernment, with courage. Because there we will see the real price of abandoning the foundation—and the door God still keeps open for restoration. When the walls fall, truth begins. And when truth begins, change begins.

Chapter Eight

What Awaits Us as a Nation

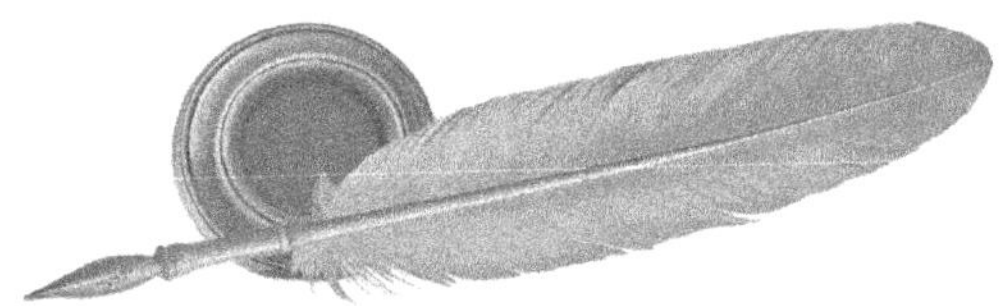

Above all that we have discussed, an inevitable question arises: **What awaits us as a nation?** I do not like being pessimistic, but I must be honest: things will not improve; they will go from bad to worse. When the United States decided to turn its back on God and replace the foundations that sustained it with human ideologies, the outcome was sealed—its fall is inevitable. Some of us still have faith that God might extend mercy if this nation humbled itself as others did in the Bible, from the least to the greatest. But realistically, that does not seem to be the case. Many in this nation have come to believe they are superior even to God Himself.

When the Foundations Weaken, the Fall Is Only a Matter of Time

If the foundations of a building weaken and no one repairs them, its collapse is not a possibility... it is a certainty. That is exactly what has happened to the United States. There were presidents who humbled themselves before God—like Roosevelt, who proclaimed days of fasting and prayer during the Great Depression. God heard and restored the nation. But today, instead of humility, we see pride. Instead of repentance, we see rebellion. Instead of dependence on God, we see open rejection.

The Decision That Marked a Before and After

One of the most disastrous decisions in modern history was removing prayer and Bible reading from public schools. Before that, although the nation was not perfect, there was still reverence, respect, and a moral sense passed down to new generations. The most prestigious universities—Harvard, Yale, Princeton—were founded by evangelists and pastors to train ministers of the gospel. Today, those same institutions reject the principles that gave them birth.

In 1962, in the case *Engel v. Vitale*, the Supreme Court declared unconstitutional a simple prayer recited in schools:

> **"Almighty God, we acknowledge our dependence upon You, and we beg Your blessings upon us, our parents, our teachers, and our country. Amen."**

They rejected the daily blessing of the God who had prospered this nation. They said: **"We do not need You."**

And from that day, the walls began to fall.

The Domino Effect

The following year, devotional Bible reading was banned in schools. Although technically it is still legal for a student to bring a Bible, pray, or share their faith, intimidation has made many believe otherwise.

Every decision contrary to biblical principles weakened a wall. Every law that rejected God tore down another. Every attempt to silence the name of Jesus in public spaces opened a deeper crack.

Today, only rubble remains.

The Statistics Speak for Themselves

We do not have time to analyze them all here, but a simple search reveals how:

- suicides increased
- violence skyrocketed
- immorality multiplied
- the family deteriorated
- respect for authority was lost
- juvenile delinquency increased
- mental health declined
- education collapsed

- addictions multiplied
- corruption became normalized

All of this began when the United States expelled God from its schools and public life.

The Presidents Knew the Secret

Many leaders from other nations came to study why the United States had prospered so greatly. The answer was always the same: **its roots were in the Bible.**

President Eisenhower expressed it this way:

- "Without God, there could be no American form of government."
- "The dignity of man is rooted in a faith deeply embedded in God."
- "The freedom of the citizen and the freedom of the believer are mutually dependent."

He even warned about the "domino effect": when one wall falls, the others follow.

That is exactly what has happened to this nation.

A Warning Congress Ignored

After the Columbine massacre, Darryl Scott—the father of one of the victims—testified before Congress:

"You have removed our heritage. You consider a simple prayer illegal. And now you ask 'why?' What we need is God."

But they did not listen.

And today we continue paying the price.

Where Is the United States in Biblical Prophecy?

Nowhere does it appear as a world power. That means that by the time of final prophetic fulfillment, the United States will no longer be the influential nation it once was. It will be weakened, irrelevant, or devastated.

The fall is imminent.

The United States has weakened its walls, eroded its foundations, and extinguished the light that once distinguished it among the nations. But although this reality is painful, it is not the end.

Every time God allows the walls to fall, it is not to destroy... it is to awaken. It is to shake. It is to call His people back to the foundation they abandoned.

Because when the walls fall, what truly sustains a nation is exposed: **its relationship with God.**

Looking Ahead

Chapter 8 showed us how we arrived here. Chapter 9 will show us what is expected of the Church in times of crisis.

Because even though the nation has chosen to turn its back on God, the Church still has a responsibility. It still has a mission. It still has a voice. It still has a calling.

Prepare to enter Chapter 9. There, we will discover that although the nation's walls lie in ruins, the spiritual walls can still be rebuilt. Let us move to the next chapter. God has more to say.

Chapter Nine
Revival

Years ago, when people spoke about the "new world order" or the "great reset," many were terrified. Others mocked it, calling it an absurd conspiracy. Some insisted that such a thing could never happen. But today, it is no longer taboo. Today it is spoken of openly, proudly, as if it were an inevitable advancement. And the most alarming part is that it has already begun, although most have not realized it. Unfortunately, we do not have space to break down every detail, but I can tell you something with absolute certainty: **if you love God and remain faithful, you have nothing to fear.** Everything that is happening is exactly what God said would happen. Do not fear, but prepare yourself and warn your family before it is too late. Do not allow the system to blind them or remove from their hearts what you have sown with tears.

A Repentance That Is No Longer Repentance

Many quote the famous passage: "If My people humble themselves..." But we no longer do it with tears, with crying, with brokenness. We repeat it like an automatic slogan—without pain, without conviction, without genuine repentance.

True repentance is what Nehemiah demonstrated: inconsolable weeping, deep conviction, and a desperate desire to make things right with God. That kind of repentance transforms nations. That kind of repentance stops judgments. That kind of repentance brings revival.

But today, many want blessings without obedience, promises without commitment, restoration without surrender. Sadly, what in many mass gatherings is called "revival" is nothing more than entertainment and the endorsement of false idols —placing man at the center instead of God Himself.

We have created a god "in my likeness" instead of conforming ourselves to His image and likeness as He created us. We have designed an individual god for each person according to the desires of our own hearts.

REVIVAL

One early morning, while praying for a great revival, I fell into that state between sleep and wakefulness. There, God showed me a vision.

I saw an abandoned house. We entered and began to clean rubble and ruins. As I watched from the doorway, I heard clearly a voice saying, **"William Fisher, greatly used in the 70s."**

I woke up immediately. I began to research him and found writings from the 1950s through 1966. As I read them, the anointing was so intense that tears streamed down my face. I felt the glory of God in every line. And I understood something profound: what this man wrote nearly 60 years ago is being fulfilled today, word for word.

It was not a message full of "new revelation" or codes to decipher. It was not a presumptuous prophetic discourse or a decorated message meant to impress. It was the pure gospel. Holiness. Repentance. Truth. A simple message, without embellishment, yet filled with such sacred anointing that it brought me to my knees. **That is precisely what we lack today.**

God continues using hidden voices to awaken entire generations.

The Cry for Revival

My heart breaks every time I think of the revival God longs to pour out over this nation. I feel spiritual birth pains. I agonize in prayer. I cry out for my city, for this nation, for the entire world.

The fields are white. The harvest is ready. Heaven is prepared. But **we ourselves are stopping God's visitation.**

Not because of a lack of power. Not because of a lack of promises. But because of a lack of unity, holiness, repentance, and obedience.

Why Satan Hates Revival

Satan fears revival because he knows that when God visits a nation:

- hearts turn back to Him
- laws align with righteousness
- society is transformed
- education changes
- corruption retreats
- families are restored
- the Church awakens
- truth shines

The great revivals of history—including those that shaped this nation—were the driving force behind:

- the abolition of slavery,
- independence,
- social justice,
- moral reform,
- the expansion of the gospel.

Revival does not depend on a man. It is a divine decree. But God responds to the cry of a humble people. **Revival has already begun, but it cannot manifest in its fullness**

until repentance reaches the deepest places of the heart.
Prayer does not produce revival.

Prayer *is* revival.

The Church Contaminated by Humanism

Without realizing it, we have been dragged by the enemy's lies. We have become humanistic Christians. We have displaced God from the center and placed ourselves there. It no longer matters what God thinks, but what we feel.

We want to defend our rights while trampling on the rights of others. We say we love God, yet we sow hatred. We say we obey His Word, yet we violate His commandments. We say we are light, yet we live in darkness.

And worst of all, we have allowed the media to shape our conscience.

We have been contaminated with:

- hatred
- racism
- intolerance
- rebellion
- disrespect for authority
- division
- pride
- arrogance

How far will we go? How can God entrust this generation with the greatest revival if we are in this condition?

An Urgent Call to the Church

Ministers, leaders, Christians: let us humble ourselves before God. Let us ask forgiveness for allowing hatred to divide us. Let us not participate in verbal violence, racism, or political contempt. It does not matter if we do not think alike. Let us respect. Let us love. Let us be the change the world needs to see.

Let us influence others—not with hatred, but with passion for the presence of God.

A National Cry

Let us declare this time as the beginning of a divine visitation. We know that in many places revival is breaking out in glory and God is doing wonderful things. Yet in many other places, there is great resistance. Let us not care who gets the credit—what matters is Him. What matters is that God moves, that His presence touches, frees, heals, and transforms this rising generation. Our children, our youth, and the new generation need to see the power of God. They need a supernatural encounter. They need a real revival. That is why I make this call.

Join the *Noon Watch*

Every day, from 12:00 to 1:00 PM, join *The Noon Watch*: pray, intercede, and cry out for a national visitation. We need

God now more than ever. Do it with your family, congregation, friends, or individually—but cry out. If you cannot choose this hour, choose another, but do it. Prayer is the only thing that will break the yoke, shatter chains, and awaken the spirit of the valiant who have not bowed their knees to Baal.

Revival begins with you. It begins with me. It begins with a surrendered heart. The prophecies are fulfilled. The world stage is set. Darkness advances. The nation trembles. The Church is being shaken. And heaven is watching.

But in the midst of all this, God has not stopped speaking. He has not stopped warning. He has not stopped calling. He has not stopped preparing His remnant.

Because even though the world is in chaos, **God still has a plan.** And His plan includes His Church—and we are part of that Church. Tune your ear to hear the voice of God and discern His plan for your life.

Chapter Ten

When Darkness Increases, the Light Must Shine Brighter

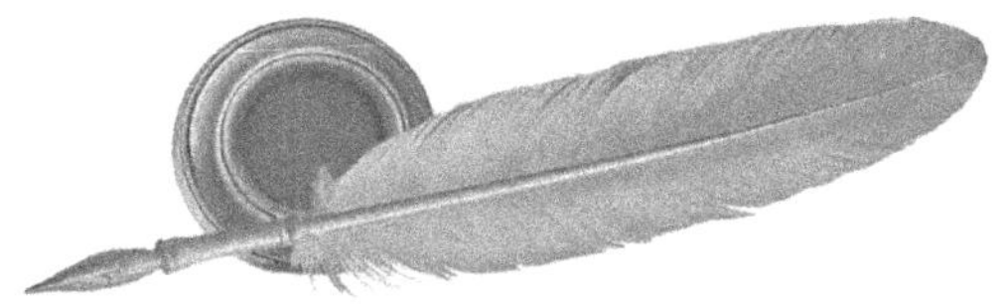

We are living in a time when darkness no longer hides. Before, evil disguised itself, concealed itself, justified itself. Today, it is celebrated. Promoted. Legislated. Applauded.

- What was once shameful is now pride.
- What was once sin is now identity.
- What was once immoral is now "progress."
- What was once dangerous is now "freedom."

And while society redefines truth, the Church faces the greatest test of its modern history: **Will we be light in the midst of darkness, or will we adapt to it?**

A Generation That Does Not Know the Foundation

The generation rising today does not know the foundations that once sustained this nation. They do not know true history. They do not know the Word. They do not know the truth. They do not know God.

Not because they cannot know Him, but because we have handed them a world without foundation:

- Schools without prayer
- Families without an altar
- Churches without fire
- Governments without the fear of God
- Media without morality
- Culture without limits
- Hearts without conviction

And when a generation grows without foundation, it grows without direction. And when it grows without direction, it becomes easy prey for deception.

The Age of Confusion

Today we live in the age of confusion:

- Confusion of identity
- Confusion of purpose
- Confusion of morality
- Confusion of authority
- Confusion of truth

The Bible said it clearly:

"In the last days, what is evil will be called good, and what is good will be called evil."

That time is no longer the future. It is present.

And as confusion advances, the Church faces a decision:

Will we be a prophetic voice or a cultural echo?

The Church at the Crossroads

The Church today stands at a critical point. Not because of a lack of resources. Not because of a lack of technology. Not because of a lack of platforms. Not because of a lack of buildings.

But because of a lack of:

- Conviction
- Holiness
- Repentance
- Discernment
- Unity
- Courage
- Fire
- Obedience

We have confused activity with revival. Emotion with transformation. Crowds with maturity. Programs with presence. And while the Church entertains itself, the enemy advances.

The War Is Not Political—It Is Spiritual

Many believe the battle we face is political. But politics is only the reflection of a deeper war.

The real battle is:

- for the hearts of our children,
- or the minds of our youth,
- for the morality of our society,
- for the truth of the Word,
- for the spiritual freedom of the nation.

It is not a war of parties—it is a war of principalities.
Not a war of ideologies—it is a war of identities.
Not a war of laws—it is a war of foundations.

The Remnant God Is Raising

Despite the darkness, God always has a remnant. A small but faithful group. People who do not bow to culture. People who do not negotiate the truth. A people who cannot be bought. People who do not remain silent. A people who do not surrender.

This remnant is not perfect, but it is obedient. Not numerous, but powerful. Not famous, but effective. Not applauded, but backed by heaven. And it is precisely this remnant that God is calling to rise.

If you can identify with that remnant, then this book is for you. I am not speaking of religiosity disguised as "holiness," but of hearts fully surrendered to Him—hearts that live to please Him, hear Him, and obey Him without reservation.

A Call to Today's Church

This chapter is not to point fingers. It is to awaken.

Not to condemn. It is to confront.

Not to frighten. It is to prepare.

God is calling His Church to:

- return to the altar
- return to the Word
- return to repentance
- return to holiness
- return to service
- return to love
- return to the fear of God

Because Revival does not begin in the White House. It begins in the home of the believer. It does not begin in Congress. It begins in the heart. It does not begin in the culture. It begins in the Church.

While I was in church on a Super Bowl Sunday, I experienced something that shook my heart. We were worshiping the Lord, preparing the atmosphere to start the service and exalt His name, when suddenly I felt the Holy Spirit whisper to me with deep sorrow:

"Today, there are 'Christians' who are more excited about the halftime show than about My presence."

Those words pierced me. I felt His sadness, His weeping, His grief. I have nothing against any artist—even though many have given their soul to the enemy—because I know the power of God can reach them. But what I cannot understand is how so many believers allow themselves to be deceived, how they lack the discernment to see what is right before their eyes.

How can a Christian support someone who uses the flag, patriotism, or culture as a disguise to lead multitudes into darkness? How can those who call themselves "the people of God" applaud human idols who mock Jesus, drag our youth to the edge of destruction, and make pacts with darkness to destroy generations?

The irony is that I know people extremely strict in their "external holiness," shaped by rules and appearances, yet they celebrate these modern idols. And when confronted, they respond: "It's cultural."

Really? That is the excuse? That is the justification? That is why we are where we are. Doesn't Scripture say:

"Have no fellowship with the unfruitful works of darkness, but rather expose them" (Ephesians 5:11)?

Do we apply the Word only when it benefits us and ignore it when it confronts our desires? God has mercy on us.

Wake Up, Church

Wake up from the sleep of indifference. Do not be deceived. Do not allow evil to influence your heart. Do not hand over your children, your grandchildren, and the next generation to the enemy simply because someone uses your flag, your culture, or your music as a disguise. Do not give your children to Molech, as ancient nations did when they turned away from God. Guard your home. Guard your faith. Guard your spiritual legacy.

The Moment Is Now

We cannot wait any longer. We cannot remain asleep. We cannot remain indifferent. We cannot remain lukewarm. Darkness is advancing. But **light always overcomes darkness.** God is looking for men and women who will say:

"Here I am, Lord. Use me."

Because when darkness increases, **the light must shine brighter.**

Chapter Evelen
The Prophetic Time: Signs, Shakings, and the Final Call

We are living in days when prophecies have ceased to be distant echoes and have become headlines. The prophetic clock advances without stopping. What once seemed impossible is now normalized. What was once denounced as exaggeration is now legislated. What was once called conspiracy is now executed as a global strategy. What was once preached as the future is now breathed as the present. And although many do not perceive it, we are experiencing an unprecedented spiritual acceleration. The days we live in do not feel like the days of the past. The prophecies we once heard from pulpits no longer sound distant; now they appear in the news. What once seemed exaggerated is now approved in laws. What once seemed impossible is now part of daily life. And while the world continues its course, I cannot ignore the sense that something is accelerating.

I remember when, nearly twenty years ago, I had a vision that marked me deeply. I saw enemy planes approaching, heard explosions, and smelled smoke. A voice from heaven gave me a date—not the year, but the day and month. When the vision ended, I became upset. I could not understand why God would show me something like that if I was not a pastor or a well-known leader at that moment. I wrote down what I could, though my frustration caused me to lose some details. It was not a dream—it was real.

Later, broken, I asked the Lord to confirm whether it was real. And He did. He showed me another vision: a train speeding forward, bombs falling on both sides, a screen showing the news of the attack, and the face of the leader of an enemy nation. I do not know when it will happen. But I know God spoke. And I know that a nation that turns away from God will inevitably face consequences. Scripture shows it again and again. Even so, for those who love the Lord, these things should not paralyze us—they should awaken us.

Today more than ever,
God is calling His people to awaken.
Not to fear, but to discern.
Not to run, but to prepare.
Not to speculate, but to live in holiness.
Prophecies were not given to entertain us,

but to alert us.
Not to create panic,
but to produce repentance.
Not to feed curiosity,
but to ignite conviction.
The world accelerates,
but so does the purpose of God.
Darkness advances, but the
Light of the Gospel shines brighter.
Judgment approaches,
but so does redemption.
For those who love God,
this is not a time to sleep.
It is a time to watch.
To trim the lamps.
To lift our eyes.
To be ready.
Because the One who
promised to come...
Is Coming.

The World vs. The Church

1. The World Is Changing Faster Than the Church Is Awakening

The speed at which the world is changing is alarming. Each day brings a new agenda, a new law, a new ideology, a new crisis, a new threat. But the most concerning part is not the speed of the world... but the slowness of the Church. While the world runs, the Church walks. While the enemy advances, the Church watches. While darkness organizes, the Church divides. While the system prepares, the Church distracts itself. And yet, God continues speaking. Continues warning. Continues calling. Continues awakening His remnant.

2. The Signs Are Right in Front of Us

Jesus said there would be clear signs before the end:

- wars and rumors of wars
- nations rising against nations
- earthquakes
- plagues
- false teachers
- increase of wickedness
- love growing cold
- persecution
- confusion
- deception
- division
- spiritual darkness

You do not need to be a theologian to see that all of this is already here. But the most evident sign is not in the world... **it is in the Church.** Jesus said, *"When you see these things, lift your heads."* He did not say: "Panic." "Hide your faith." "Silence your voice." "Adapt to the system." He said, **"Lift**

your heads." Meaning: awaken, discern, prepare, stand firm.

3. The Shaking Is Not Punishment—It Is Mercy

Many see shakings as judgment. But for the children of God, shakings are mercy.

God shakes in order to:

- awaken
- purify
- separate
- correct
- align
- prepare
- strengthen
- reveal
- restore

The shaking does not destroy the remnant. It awakens it. Positions it. Activates it. The shaking is not the end. It is the beginning of something new.

4. The Remnant Is Being Trained in Silence

God is raising a remnant that does not seek platforms, applause, fame, or recognition. It is a remnant that has been processed in:

- the desert

- solitude
- prayer
- brokenness
- obedience
- intercession
- intimacy with God

It is a remnant that does not sell out. Do not fear. Does not compromise. Does not conform. Does not surrender. It is a remnant that understands the battle is not political—it is spiritual. That the war is not against flesh and blood. That victory does not come from human strategies, but from the Holy Spirit.

5. The Final Call: Prepare the Way

This chapter is not to frighten. It is to prepare. Not to alarm. It is to awaken. Not to divide. It is to unite the remnant. God is calling His Church to:

- return to the altar
- return to the Word
- return to fasting
- return to intercession
- return to holiness
- return to obedience
- return to first love

Because before the final judgment comes, a final revival will come. A revival that will not be emotional, but spiritual.

Not superficial, but deep. Not local, but global. Not of crowds, but of surrendered hearts. And God is seeking those willing to prepare the way.

6. Do Not Fear: God Is in Control

Even if the world trembles, even if nations shake, even if the economy collapses, even if morality crumbles, even if darkness advances...

God is still seated on His throne.

He has not lost control. He has not changed His plan. He has not canceled His promises. He has not abandoned His people. And **He is with you.**

Chapter Twelve

The Final Call: Preparing for What Is Coming

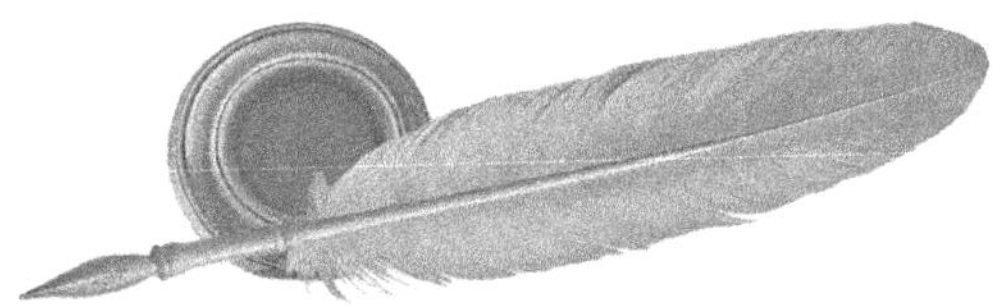

We have reached the final chapter of this book, and under no circumstances do we intend to cause panic with what we are sharing. **We are simply exposing truths that, for many years, have been known, but that today God is urgently bringing back to our remembrance.** If, after reading this book, we simply remain with our arms crossed, indifferent, doing nothing about it, then we have wasted our time reading it. Throughout this book, we have spoken about fallen walls, moral decay, the indifference of the Church, the prophetic time we are living in, and the revival God longs to pour out. But now we arrive at the most important point of the entire message:

- **What must we do?**
- **How do we prepare?**
- **What does God expect from us in this final hour?**

Because it is not enough to discern the season. It is not enough to understand the signs. It is not enough to recognize the darkness. It is not enough to lament the condition of the nation.

God did not call us to be spectators of chaos. He called us to be participants in His purpose.

1. Return to the Altar: The Place Where Everything Begins

The altar is not a piece of furniture. It is a lifestyle. It is the place where:

- pride is broken
- rebellion melts
- the heart is purified
- vision is renewed
- direction is received
- passion is restored
- the fire is ignited

The Church lost power when it lost the altar. The family lost unity when it lost the altar. The nation lost direction when it lost the altar. If we want to see revival, we must return to the altar—not an emotional altar, but an altar of total surrender.

2. Return to the Word: The Truth That Does Not Change

We live in a generation that has replaced the Bible with:

- opinions
- emotions
- ideologies
- social media
- human philosophies

But the Word remains:

- the sword
- the lamp
- the foundation
- the compass
- the voice of God

We cannot face a prophetic time with a superficial faith. We need a faith anchored in the Word.

3. Return to Holiness: The Mark of the Remnant

Holiness is not perfection. It is a separation. It is obedience. It is purity of heart. It is living to please God, not people.

The Church lost authority when it lost holiness. The enemy does not fear a large Church. He fears a **holy** Church.

4. Return to Intercession: The Warfare That Changes History

Intercession is not a beautiful prayer. It is spiritual warfare. It is standing in the gap. It is weeping for those who do not weep. It is crying out for those who do not cry out. It is fighting for those who do not know how to fight.

God has always saved nations because of intercessors:

- Abraham interceded for Sodom.
- Moses interceded for Israel.
- Daniel interceded for his people.
- Nehemiah interceded for his nation.
- The early Church interceded for Peter.

Today, God is seeking intercessors willing to say: **"Here I am, Lord. Send me."**

5. Return to Service: Revival Is Not a Show

- Revival is not an event. It is a responsibility.
- It is not to entertain the Church. It is to mobilize it.
- It is not to fill buildings. It is to empty hell.
- It is not to create celebrities. It is to raise servants.
- God is not looking for talent. He is looking for availability.

6. Return to First Love: The Flame That Should Never Have Gone Out

First love is not emotion. It is priority. It is surrender. It is passion. It is obedience. It is intimacy. Jesus told the Church of Ephesus: **"You have left your first love."** He did not say: "You lost it." He said: "You left it." What is left can be recovered.

7. Prepare for the Shaking and for the Glory

The time ahead will be difficult. But it will also be glorious for those who obey God and walk in His principles, commandments, and statutes.

There will be:

- more darkness
- more confusion
- more persecution
- more deception
- more division

But there will also be:

- more revival
- more miracles
- more salvation
- more visitation
- more glory

The same God who allowed the shaking will allow the restoration. The same God who allowed the walls to fall will raise new walls. The same God who allowed the crisis will release His glory.

CONCLUSION
THE REMNANT THAT WILL CHANGE HISTORY

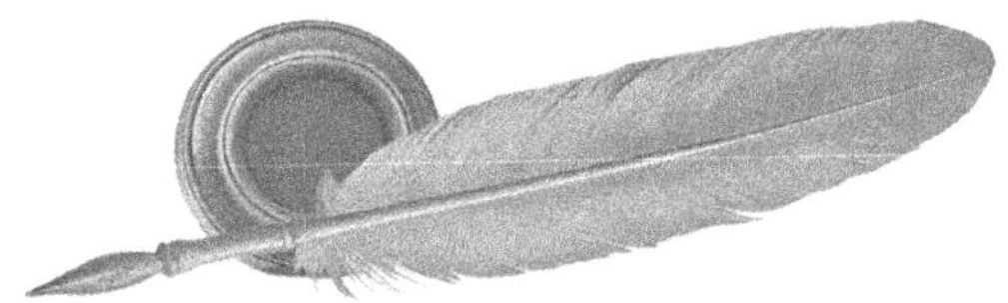

This book is not a political analysis. It is not a social commentary. It is not a historical study. **It is a prophetic call. A cry from heaven. A spiritual trumpet. A divine warning. An urgent awakening.** The United States has fallen. Its walls are in ruins. Its foundations are broken. Its morality is collapsing. Its identity is being destroyed. **But God is not finished.** God never finishes with a nation as long as there is a remnant that cries out. As long as there is a people who pray. As long as there is a Church that humbles itself. As long as there are hearts that surrender. As long as there are knees that bow. As long as there are voices that refuse to be silenced. God does not need crowds. He needs a remnant. And that remnant is **you**. That remnant is **us**. That remnant is the Church that does not negotiate truth. The Church that does not sell out. The Church that does not surrender. The Church that does not become contaminated. The Church that does not conform. The Church that is not ashamed of the gospel.

Although many have allowed themselves to be contaminated, God is raising a generation that is:

- rebuilding walls
- restoring foundations
- igniting altars
- awakening nations
- preparing the way of the Lord

Because what is coming for many
will be destruction...
But for the remnant...
It will be Glory.
It will not be defeat...
It is revival.
It will not be silence...
It is a prophetic voice.
What is coming will not be fear...
It is spiritual authority.
What is coming will not be
darkness for the Church...
It is light in the midst of darkness.

And the Lord says:
**"Arise, shine, for your light has come,
and the glory of the Lord has risen upon you."**
—Isaiah 60:1

This is the time.
This is the call.
This is the moment.

Do not look at the chaos.
Look at the promise.
Do not look at the fall.
Look at the restoration.
Do not look at the darkness.
Look at the glory that is coming.
Because even if the nation trembles,
God is still God.
And He will fulfill His purpose.

Final Prayer for the Nation

A Prayer for the United States in Times of Crisis and Restoration

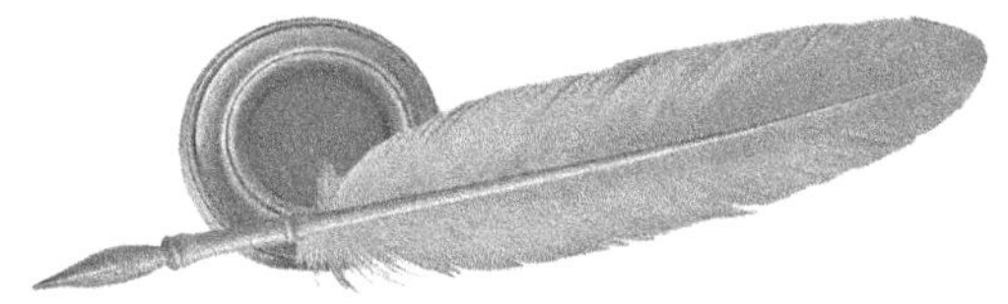

Heavenly Father,

Almighty God, Creator of heaven and earth, we acknowledge that You are the Supreme Judge of the Universe. Today, we come before You as a nation, as a people, as Your children, recognizing that without You, we are nothing and can do nothing. Lord, we confess that this nation has turned away from Your ways. We have allowed the injustice of man to rule, legislate, and exercise authority based on humanistic laws and not on Your Word. We have been cruel. We have mocked Your precepts and commandments, believing they were outdated, powerless, and obsolete. We have built walls without a foundation. We have replaced Your truth with human opinions, and we have allowed darkness to advance while the Church remained silent.

But today, Father, we humble ourselves before You.

We cry out for mercy. We cry out for forgiveness. We cry out for restoration. We declare that from this day forward, our lives will never be the same. We will rise and rebuild. We will return to our first love, to the first works, to obedience and holiness.

Lord, we ask forgiveness for Congress, for the Senate, and for every executive branch and authority that governs this nation. We confess the sins of hatred, contempt, abuse, corruption, and disloyalty.

Forgive every atrocity committed—even in the name of faith, social justice, or the powers entrusted to us.

Heal our land. Awaken Your Church. Ignite a genuine revival. Raise a remnant full of fire. Open the eyes of the blind. Soften hardened hearts. Restore the spiritual walls that have been torn down. Lord, pour out Your Spirit over our children, over our youth, over our families, over our leaders, over our cities, over our schools, and over our government officials.

May the light of Christ shine again over this nation. May truth be truth again. May justice be justice again. May holiness be holiness again. May the Church be the Church again.

Father, do not allow the enemy to write the final chapter of this nation. Write the final story Yourself. Lift Your mighty hand. Do what only You can do. And while we wait for Your intervention, make us faithful, courageous, obedient, and filled with the Holy Spirit.

Today, we surrender before You, recognizing that You reign in power. You are the King of kings and Lord of lords. Your kingdom is everlasting. Even the most powerful on earth will bow and worship You. Therefore, today we bow before You and lay our crowns at Your beautiful and mighty presence. Thank You for not forgetting us. Thank You for loving us. Thank You for redeeming us. In the name of Jesus—the only King, the only Lord, the only Savior—we pray.

Amen

Prophetic Epilogue
A Legacy for the Coming Generation

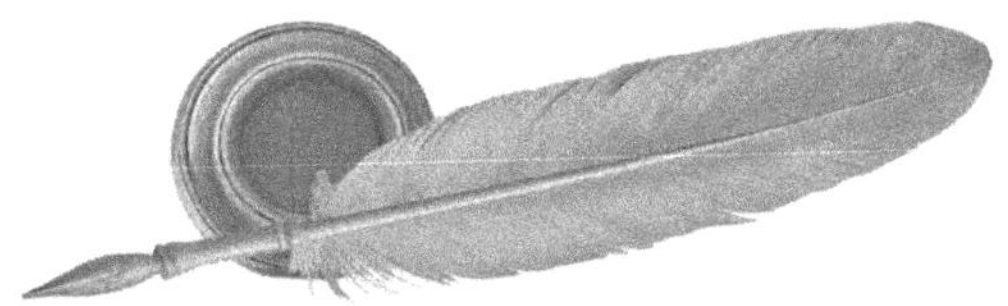

I love with all my heart this nation that welcomed me and where I have been blessed, strengthened, prepared, and formed. In this land, I met the man with whom I joined my life, and this year we celebrate thirty-five years of marriage. Here, my four treasures were born—the most beautiful gifts God has given us. Here I obtained my first job, and here I have lived the last decades of my life. Many years ago, when my daughters were little, and I drove them to school each morning, I experienced something that marked my spirit forever. As I was driving, my eyes became fixed on the license plate of the vehicle in front of me. It wasn't the first time I had seen it—I saw it every day—but that day was not a coincidence. That day, God wanted to speak to me. The Massachusetts license plates carry the words *The Spirit of America*, and as I looked at them, I felt the Holy Spirit minister to me with a mixture of tenderness and sorrow.

"Do you know why that is there?" He whispered to my heart. "Because this is where the American nation began. This is where the gospel entered. This is where the Spirit convicted of sin, brought deliverance and healing. Here began the spiritual prosperity of the gospel of Jesus Christ."

But what happens if that Spirit departs? What happens if this nation opens its doors to other spirits—to false gods, to deceiving spirits, to the spirit of the enemy? Then *The Spirit of America* will no longer be the Spirit of God. Let us ensure that the spirit of this nation remains the Spirit of God. Teach your children and the generations to come, because if they do not know the true God, they will grow up without spiritual identity.

That morning, I understood that the battle for a nation begins in the heart of families, in the formation of children, in the transmission of spiritual legacy.

And as if God wanted to affirm it even more, days later, I experienced something that sealed my heart. On my way home after dropping my daughter off at school, I passed a traffic light where several volunteers were campaigning for their candidate. It was the middle of winter; the cold cut through the skin. Yet there they were—firm, with gloves, hats, and signs in hand, passionately defending the one who represented their ideals. As I turned right, I thought, *"Wow!*

In this freezing cold, and they don't care. They're here, faithful to their candidate, at this hour of the morning."

In that moment, I heard the voice of the Holy Spirit—soft, yet filled with sorrow:

"And who will do it for Jesus? Who's going to stand for Jesus?"

I felt His tears. I felt His pain. And I began to weep as I drove. That whisper broke something inside me and ignited a stirring that led me to seek His presence more intensely than ever before.

That is why—precisely because I love this nation deeply—I have obeyed the voice of God in writing this book. I wrote it many years ago, but it was not until now that He said to me, **"It is time."**

This book does not end here. After so many years kept away, today God allows me to publish it. My prayer is that it awakens in you the same fire He ignited within me: a fire that burns for true revival, a passion for His presence that consumes me, a holy dissatisfaction that refuses to conform to the status quo.

Because God is not finished with this nation, nor with His Church, nor with you. Although in my lifetime I believe we are walking through the darkest stage of moral and spiritual decline, I also believe we are living the most glorious time for those who embrace His Word, His principles, and His statutes. It is a time when darkness advances, yes—but also a time when the light of God shines with greater intensity, illuminating those who are still sensitive to His voice. A time when the walls fall, but also a time when God raises up repairers of the breach. A time when many grow cold, but also a time when God continues awakening His remnant.

This epilogue is not a closing. It is an assignment. It is a call.

God is raising men and women who will not conform, who will not surrender, who will not sell out, who will not remain silent.

Men and women who will rebuild the spiritual walls of this nation. Who will restore the altar? Who will ignite revival? Who will prepare the way of the Lord? And you, reader, are not here by coincidence. God chose you for this time. For this generation. For this battle. For this revival.

May this book be an eternal reminder that even when the walls fall, God always raises a remnant that changes history.

Let us make sure we are part of that remnant.

Author's Note

Edna L. Isaac

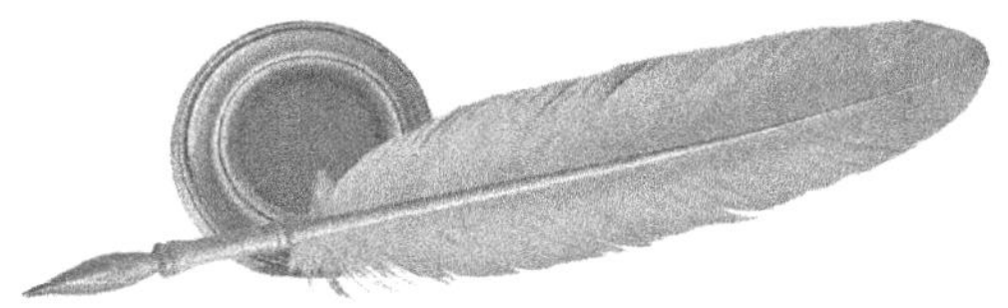

Writing this book has been one of the most challenging, transformative, and sacred processes of my life. It was not born from an intellectual idea, nor from a personal desire, nor from a human agenda. It was born from a spiritual burden—from nights of prayer, from tears shed for this nation, from visions that marked my spirit, and from a calling I could not ignore.

Each chapter was written with reverent fear, with responsibility, with brokenness, and with the deep conviction that God still speaks, still warns, still awakens, and still calls His people to return to Him. Many years have passed in the process of writing it, and I did not write these pages to point fingers, but to awaken. Not to condemn, but to confront with love. Not to sow fear, but to ignite hope.

Not to divide, but to unite the remnant. Not to exalt a nation, but to exalt the God who can restore it.

My deepest desire is that this book has led you to reflect, to examine your heart, to look at the spiritual condition of our nation, and above all, to listen to the voice of the Holy Spirit in the midst of these turbulent times.

If there is something I have learned while writing these pages, it is that:

- God never abandons His people
- God always has a remnant
- God always sends warnings before judgment
- God always offers mercy before the fall
- God always raises voices when darkness increases

And you, reader, are part of that story. You are part of that remnant. You are part of that calling.

My prayer is that these words will not remain as ink on paper, but that they become action, intercession, repentance, courage, and obedience. That they awaken within you an inner fire—the fire of the Holy Spirit, the same fire that dwelled in Jesus during His ministry and today through the Holy Spirit in every believer who chooses to be sensitive to His voice. That they move you to rebuild the spiritual walls of your life, your family, your church, and your nation. That they remind you that even when times are difficult, God is still God, and His purpose cannot be stopped.

Thank you for allowing me to enter your heart through these pages. Thank you for walking with me on this spiritual journey. Thank you for being part of what God is doing in this generation.

With love, reverence, and hope,

Edna L. Isaac

References

Adams, J. (1776–1826). *The Adams Papers*. Massachusetts Historical Society.

American Memory Collection. (n.d.). Library of Congress. https://www.loc.gov

The Atlantic. (n.d.). Contemporary Culture Articles. https://www.theatlantic.com

Barna Group. (n.d.). *Faith & Culture Research*. https://www.barna.com

Beacon Bible Commentary. (1967). Beacon Hill Press.

Bible Society. (1960). *Holy Bible, Reina-Valera 1960*. United Bible Societies.

Britannica, Encyclopaedia. (n.d.). *U.S. History*. https://www.britannica.com

Cambridge University Press. (n.d.). *Political Thought Series*.

Census Bureau, U.S. (n.d.). *Demographic and Social Data*. https://www.census.gov

Constitution of the United States of America. (1787). National Archives.

Declaration of Independence of the United States. (1776). National Archives.

Holman Bible Dictionary. (n.d.). Holman Reference.

Hamilton, A., Madison, J., & Jay, J. (1788). *The Federalist Papers*. National Archives.

Federal Bureau of Investigation. (n.d.). *Uniform Crime Reports*. https://www.fbi.gov

Gallup. (n.d.). *Public Opinion Research*. https://www.gallup.com

Grudem, W. (1994). *Systematic Theology*. Zondervan.

Harvard Kennedy School. (n.d.). *Democracy & Governance Studies*.

Henry, M. (1706). *Commentary on the Whole Bible*.

History.com. . (n.d.). *U.S. Presidents & Founding Era*. https://www.history.com

John Adams Papers. (n.d.). Massachusetts Historical Society.

Library of Congress. (n.d.). *Government Documents*. https://www.loc.gov

Massachusetts Historical Society. (n.d.). *Founders' Documents.*

Moody Bible Commentary. (n.d.). Moody Publishers.

Mount Vernon Ladies' Association. (n.d.). *George Washington Papers.* https://www.mountvernon.org

National Archives and Records Administration (NARA). (n.d.). https://www.archives.gov

The New York Times. (n.d.). *Politics & Society.* https://www.nytimes.com

Oxford Research Encyclopedia. (n.d.). *American History.* Oxford University Press.

Orr, J. E. (1975). *The Rebirth of Revival.*

Pew Research Center. (n.d.). *Religion & Public Life.* https://www.pewresearch.org

RealClearPolitics. (n.d.). *Political Trends.* https://www.realclearpolitics.com

Ryrie, C. (1999). *Basic Theology.* Moody Publishers.

Smithsonian Institution. (n.d.). *American History Collections.*

Tozer, A. W. (1950). *The Pursuit of God.*

U.S. House of Representatives – Office of the Historian. (n.d.). https://history.house.gov

U.S. Senate Historical Office. (n.d.). https://www.senate.gov

Walvoord, J. F. (1974). *The Prophecy Knowledge Handbook.*

The Washington Post. (n.d.). *Politics & Culture.* https://www.washingtonpost.com

White House Historical Association. (n.d.). *Presidential History & White House Facts.* https://www.whitehousehistory.org

www.ingramcontent.com/pod-product-compliance
Lightning Source LLC
Chambersburg PA
CBHW050005040726
47599CB00014B/1222